高等职业教育"十三五"规划教材

PRACTICAL ENGLISH COURSE

实用英语综合教程（上）

练习册
WORKBOOK

主　编　洪　玲　向中平
副主编　谭　怡　吴　靓
参　编　李　龙　崔永琦　罗　粲
　　　　宋津晶　罗　霞

北京理工大学出版社
BEIJING INSTITUTE OF TECHNOLOGY PRESS

版权专有 侵权必究

图书在版编目（CIP）数据

实用英语综合教程（上）练习册 / 洪玲，向中平主编 . —北京：北京理工大学出版社，2017.7
（2018.7 重印）

ISBN 978 – 7 – 5682 – 4475 – 6

Ⅰ . ①实… Ⅱ . ①洪… ②向… Ⅲ . ①英语 – 高等职业教育 – 习题集 Ⅳ . ①H319.6

中国版本图书馆 CIP 数据核字（2017）第 182184 号

出版发行 / 北京理工大学出版社有限责任公司
社　　址 / 北京市海淀区中关村南大街 5 号
邮　　编 / 100081
电　　话 /（010）68914775（总编室）
　　　　　（010）82562903（教材售后服务热线）
　　　　　（010）68948351（其他图书服务热线）
网　　址 / http： // www.bitpress.com.cn
经　　销 / 全国各地新华书店
印　　刷 / 北京虎彩文化传播有限公司
开　　本 / 787 毫米 × 1092 毫米　1/16
印　　张 / 7　　　　　　　　　　　　　　　　　　　　　责任编辑 / 武丽娟
字　　数 / 168 千字　　　　　　　　　　　　　　　　　　文案编辑 / 武丽娟
版　　次 / 2017 年 7 月第 1 版　2018 年 7 月第 2 次印刷　　责任校对 / 周瑞红
定　　价 / 29.80 元　　　　　　　　　　　　　　　　　　责任印制 / 李志强

图书出现印装质量问题，请拨打售后服务热线，本社负责调换

前 言

本书是《实用英语教程》开发的配套教学用书，是根据《高职高专教育英语课程教学基本要求》，围绕提高高职学生的英语应用能力而编写的，充分考虑到高职学生的现有英语水平，本着实用为主、够用为度的原则，供学生复习、操练、巩固和拓展学生用书中所学到的语言知识和技能，力图增加学生的词汇量，巩固原有基础，拓展知识面，培养学生的英语自主学习能力和提高英语实际应用能力，同时，结合高等学校英语应用能力考试的要求设计相关练习，起到实践运用的作用，为学生参加这项考试提供极好的准备素材。

本书共有 8 个单元，每单元包括听力（Listening）、词汇和语法（Vocabulary and Structure）、阅读（Reading）、翻译（Translation）、写作（Writing）。

听力：包括三个部分的练习：对话、会话和简单短文。对话、会话和短文均以日常生活和实用的交际性内容为主。

语法和词汇：旨在帮助学生复习、操练和巩固重点单词、固定搭配、句型的用法，以及相关的词形变换，动词的时态和语态等。

阅读：主要是锻炼学生从书面文字材料获取信息的能力，包括一般性阅读材料（文化、社会、常识、科普、经贸、人物等）和应用性文字，扩大学生的知识面，提高阅读技能。

翻译：一方面根据意思选择句子结构，搭起基本框架；选择适当的词汇和表达手段，特别要按英语的表达逻辑来调整语句进行选择判断；另一方面，运用汉语把英语所表达的思想准确而完整地重新表达出来的语言能力训练。

写作：参考"高等学校英语应用能力考试"的题型和内容，结合学校日常生活和学习，进行写作训练，主要通过范例，要求学生能够阅读并仿写祝贺信、感谢信、道歉信、请假条、通知、海报、邮件等多种常见的应用文。

本教材主编为洪玲、向中平，副主编为谭怡、吴靓，参加本书编写工作的编者有李龙、崔永琦、罗粲、宋津晶、罗霞。由于时间仓促，实际编写中难免出现纰漏，敬请大家在使用过程中批评指正！

编写组

2017 年 4 月

目 录

Unit 1 ·· 1
   Part Ⅰ   Listening Comprehension ··· 1
   Part Ⅱ   Vocabulary and Structure ·· 2
   Part Ⅲ   Reading Comprehension ·· 3
   Part Ⅳ   Translation ·· 8
   Part Ⅴ   Writing ·· 9

Unit 2 ·· 13
   Part Ⅰ   Listening Comprehension ··· 13
   Part Ⅱ   Vocabulary and Structure ·· 14
   Part Ⅲ   Reading Comprehension ·· 16
   Part Ⅳ   Translation ·· 22
   Part Ⅴ   Writing ·· 23

Unit 3 ·· 27
   Part Ⅰ   Listening Comprehension ··· 27
   Part Ⅱ   Vocabulary and Structure ·· 28
   Part Ⅲ   Reading Comprehension ·· 30
   Part Ⅳ   Translation ·· 35
   Part Ⅴ   Writing ·· 36

Unit 4 ·· 41
   Part Ⅰ   Listening Comprehension ··· 41
   Part Ⅱ   Vocabulary and Structure ·· 42
   Part Ⅲ   Reading Comprehension ·· 44
   Part Ⅳ   Translation ·· 47
   Part Ⅴ   Writing ·· 48

Unit 5 ·· 53
   Part Ⅰ   Listening Comprehension ··· 53

Part II	Vocabulary and Structure	54
Part III	Reading Comprehension	56
Part IV	Translation	60
Part V	Writing	60

Unit 6 65

Part I	Listening Comprehension	65
Part II	Vocabulary and Structure	66
Part III	Reading Comprehension	68
Part IV	Translation	72
Part V	Writing	73

Unit 7 77

Part I	Listening Comprehension	77
Part II	Vocabulary and Structure	78
Part III	Reading Comprehension	80
Part IV	Translation	85
Part V	Writing	86

Unit 8 90

Part I	Listening Comprehension	90
Part II	Vocabulary and Structure	91
Part III	Reading Comprehension	92
Part IV	Translation	96
Part V	Writing	97

Unit 1

Part I Listening Comprehension

Directions: *This part is to test your listening ability. It consists of 3 sections.*

Section A

Directions: *This section is to test your ability to understand short dialogues. There are 5 recorded dialogues in it. After each dialogue, there is a recorded question. Both the dialogues and questions will be spoken only once. When you hear a question, you should decide on the correct answer from the 4 choices marked A, B, C and D given in your test paper. Then you should mark the corresponding letter on the Answer Sheet with a single line through the center.*

1. A. You can take a taxi.
   C. It's about twenty miles.
   B. I'll fly to New York next week.
   D. It's only six hundred yuan.

2. A. It's very far from here.
   C. I've got a good idea.
   B. It's very small, but nice.
   D. I've been there.

3. A. I've got some paper.
   C. That's great.
   B. OK, thank you.
   D. Oh, no problem.

4. A. Sure. You take the other end.
   C. I think it's too expensive.
   B. Turn right at the next corner.
   D. I'm afraid it can't work.

5. A. I'm sorry to hear that.
   C. I like Chinese food.
   B. It's very kind of you to help me.
   D. I'd like to, but I'll have a meeting.

Section B

Directions: *This section is to test your ability to understand short conversations. There are 5 recorded conversations in it. After each conversation, there is a recorded question. Both the conversations and questions will be spoken two times. When you hear a question, you should decide on the correct answer from the 4 choices marked A, B, C and D given in your test paper. Then you should mark the corresponding letter on the Answer Sheet with a single line through the center.*

6. A. Pass a letter to Mr. Black.
   B. Talk to Mr. Black.

C. See Mr. Black. D. Ask about Mr. Black.
7. A. In a store. B. In a post office.
   C. At a restaurant. D. At a bus stop.
8. A. 9：55. B. 10：00. C. 9：50. D. 10：05.
9. A. A magazine. B. A dictionary. C. A book. D. A newspaper.
10. A. Too old. B. Too strict. C. Very quite. D. Very nice.

Section C

Directions：*In this section you will hear a recorded short passage. The passage is printed on the test paper, but with some words or phrases missing. The passage will be read three times. During the second reading, you are required to put the missing words or phrases on the Answer Sheet in order of the numbered blanks according to what you hear. The third reading is for you to check your writing. Now the passage will begin.*

John is a bus driver. He gets up at six o'clock, eats a light ___(11)___ in a hurry, and then rushes to work. He likes his job but hates to drive in bad ___(12)___. Rain and snow make the roads dangerous.

John's wife, Carol, works every day from ___(13)___ to noon as a bookkeeper. She likes keeping her house neat and tidy. She has a place for everything and throws out what she doesn't need. John is just the opposite. He ___(14)___ everything. He keeps clothes that don't ___(15)___ him any more, old magazines, boxes and papers. Nothing of his is in good order.

Part II Vocabulary and Structure

Directions：*This part is to test your ability to construct grammatically correct sentences. It consists of 2 sections.*

Section A

Directions：*In this section, there are 10 incomplete sentences. You are required to complete each one by deciding on the most appropriate word or words from the 4 choices marked A, B, C and D. Then you should mark the corresponding letter on the Answer Sheet with a single line through the center.*

16. All men have their ____ duties.
    A. respect   B. respectable   C. respectful   D. respective
17. I don't think that your watch is ____.
    A. worthy the price   B. worth the price
    C. worth   D. worth to buy
18. Students often find ____ jobs during their summer holidays.

A. temper   B. temporarily   C. temporary   D. temptation

19. A person who is ____ in learning to speak another language should learn body language as well.

    A. succeed   B. successful   C. succeeding   D. successive

20. Sarah, hurry up. I'm afraid you won't have time to ____ before the party.

    A. get changed   B. get change   C. get changing   D. get to change

21. Her son promised ____ in the bedroom until the baby stopped ____.

    A. staying, to cry   B. to stay, crying
    C. for staying, to cry   D. to stay, to cry

22. How much are you going to ____ me for repairing this bike?

    A. charge   B. request   C. need   D. require

23. He would give no ____ for his behavior.

    A. aim   B. cause   C. reason   D. target

24. That is ____ we all support his idea.

    A. what   B. why   C. where   D. when

25. ____ is troubling me is ____ I don't understand ____ he said.

    A. What; that; what   B. What; what; what
    C. That; that; what   D. Why; that; which

Section B

Directions: *There are 10 incomplete statements here. You should fill in each blank with the proper form of the word given in brackets. Write the word or words in the corresponding space on the Answer Sheet.*

26. I spoke to him ____ his behavior. (concern)
27. The ____ of air on a high mountain is bad for people with weak hearts. (rare)
28. ____ parents get their children into the best schools. (push)
29. He could not resist the ____ to drink another glass of beer. (tempt)
30. She received ____ for her many achievements. (recognize)
31. You will have to take the doctor's ____ to a chemist's. (prescribe)
32. He was elected by a ____ of 3,240 votes. (major)
33. I opened a bank account for my ____. (save)
34. My library books are a week ____. (due)
35. I know I'm only an ____ fool, but honestly, that is our only hope. (ideal)

Part Ⅲ Reading Comprehension

Directions: *This part is to test your reading ability. There are 5 tasks for you to fulfill. You should read the reading materials carefully and do the tasks as you are instructed.*

Task 1

Directions: *After reading the following passage, you will find 5 questions or unfinished statements, numbered 36 to 40. For each question or statement there are 4 choices marked A, B, C and D. You should make the correct choice and mark the corresponding letter on the Answer Sheet with a single line through the center.*

Winter-swimming has become popular in Beijing. Three years ago, few people would go swimming in the icy waters. But now, there is a winter-swimming Enthusiasts Club with more than 2,000 members. The oldest is 84 years of age and the youngest is only 7. The members are from all walks of life. They may be workers, peasants, soldiers, teachers or students.

Though it is now the coldest part of the season and the water temperature in the city's lakes is around 0℃, many winter-swimmers still swim in the icy waters, even when it is snowing. They enjoy themselves in the lake, while the people by the side of the lake are wearing heavy clothes.

Why are so many people interested in winter-swimming? Because winter-swimming can be good for one's health. Bei Sha is a good example. He is 69 years old, and he had once suffered from heart trouble for 26 years. After ten years of winter-swimming, he is now in good health. Scientists are now studying the effects of winter-swimming on health.

36. Among the winter-swimmers, the oldest man is ____ years older than the youngest one.
    A. 91 B. 84 C. 77 D. 7

37. "The members are from all walks of life" (Para. 1, L. 4) here means that ____.
    A. the members do different jobs at different places
    B. they come from all parts of Beijing
    C. they are persons of different ages
    D. they are men and women, old and young

38. The winter-swimmers are able to swim in the icy waters, even on snowy days because ____.
    A. they are not afraid of cold
    B. they often swim in the city waters and get used to it
    C. they think they can benefit from it
    D. winter-swimming can make people healthy

39. Winter-swimming has become popular in Beijing because ____.
    A. more and more people like to swim in winter
    B. it is more interesting than swimming in summer
    C. winter-swimmers are brave men
    D. winter-swimming does a lot of good to one's health

40. The best title for this passage should be ____.
    A. People in Beijing Like Swimming in Winter

B. Winter-swimming—A Craze in Beijing Stated

C. People Benefit from Winter-swimming

D. Winter-swimmers Are Brave Men

Task 2

Directions: *This task is the same as Task 1. The 5 questions or unfinished statements are numbered 41 to 45.*

For centuries, the only form of written correspondence was the letters. Letters were, and are, sent by some form of postal service, the history of which goes back a long way. Indeed, the Egyptians began sending letters from about 2000 BC, as did the Chinese, a thousand years later.

Of course, modern postal services now are much more developed and faster, depending on cars and planes for delivery as they do. Yet, they are still too slow for some people to send urgent documents and letters.

The invention of the fax machine increased the speed of delivering documents. When you send a fax, you are sending a copy of a piece of correspondence to someone by telephone service. It was not until the early 1980s that such a service was developed enough for business to be able to fax documents to each other.

Fax service is still very much in use, when copies of documents are required to be sent, but, for speedy correspondence, fax has been largely replaced by email. Email is used to describe messages sent from one computer user to another.

There are advantages and disadvantages of email. If you send someone an email, then he will receive it extremely quickly. Normal postal services are rather slow as far as speed of delivery is concerned. However, if you write something by email, which you might later regret, and send it immediately, there is no chance for second thoughts. At least, if you are posting a letter, you have to address and seal the envelope and take it to the post box. There is plenty of time to change your mind. The message is: think before you email!

41. We can learn from the passage that ____.

    A. email is less popular than fax service

    B. the postal service has over the years become faster

    C. the postal service has over the years become slower

    D. the fax service has a history as long as the postal service

42. It can be inferred from the passage that ____.

    A. the fax service had been fully developed by the 1980s

    B. letters have been used in China for about 1,000 years

    C. the fax machine was invented after the 1980s

    D. letters have been used in Egypt for about 2,000 years

43. In the last paragraph, the writer mentions "think before you email" to show that ____

　　A. you may regret if you don't seal your envelope

　　B. you may regret before you send something by email

　　C. you'd better not send your email in a hurry

　　D. you need plenty of time to send an email

44. The passage mainly deals with ____.

　　A. the progress in correspondence　　B. the advantage of fax machine

　　C. the advantage of email　　D. the invention of fax machine

45. The passage mentions ____ forms of written correspondence.

　　A. one　　　B. two　　　C. three　　　D. four

Task 3

Directions: *After reading the following passage, you will find 5 questions or unfinished statements, numbered 46 to 50. For each question or statement there are 4 choices marked A, B, C and D. You should make the correct choice and mark the corresponding letter on the Answer Sheet with a single line through the center.*

　　There is not much call for a complete working knowledge of table manners in America today. Many families only gather, all at once, around the dinner table at holiday feasts, and most restaurants are too casual to require, or even allow for more than basic good table manners. If a diner drops his napkin at a bistro (小酒店，小餐馆) he would practice proper etiquette by signaling a member of the staff to bring him a fresh one, or he would probably have to do without a napkin at all. Try as he might make eye contact and indicate the nature of the problem with a subtle (难以琢磨的) wiggle (摆动) of the eyebrow and downward flicker of the glance, he is likely to succeed only in causing his date to think he is making a play for the server. Although strict good manners forbid placing a used eating utensil back on table, the server removing a plate on which a fork has quite properly been positioned might drop that item back where it started, making more of a clatter (咔嗒声) than if the dinner had simply done it, herself.

　　From time to time—perhaps at an important business dinner, a romantic date at an expensive restaurant, or a first dinner with the family of the person who may be "the One"—it is necessary to display a more sophisticate (复杂的) knowledge of table etiquette. This is not difficult, once you have mastered the basics. Anyone armed with this core arcane (神秘的) details of etiquette (which would be quite difficult, considering the wide variation of customs in different cultures and from generation to generation), but rather to behave with graciousness and poise at the table.

46. At present, American families ____.

　　A. obey table manners　　　　B. ignore table mannners

　　C. follow traditional rules　　　D. try new rules

47. If the customer dropped his napkin at a small restaurant, he ____.

   A. must wait for the new one

   B. should pick it up and go on using it

   C. can go on with his dinner without it

   D. may tell the server directly

48. The server's attitude to table manners is ____.

   A. strict   B. worried   C. tired   D. moving

49. Sophisticated knowledge of table etiquette in business dinner is ____.

   A. essential   B. potential   C. radical   D. necessary

50. What's the purpose of the author?

   A. The author hopes people change their table manners.

   B. The author doesn't like table manners.

   C. The author urges people to fully practice table manners.

   D. The author wants to express his thoughts on graceful manners at the table.

Task 4

Directions: *The following is a list of terms related to marketing. After reading it, you are required to find the items equivalent to（与……等同）those given in Chinese in the table below. Then you should put the corresponding letters in brackets on the Answer Sheet, numbered 51 through 55.*

A—No Turn

B—On Sale or Return

C—Please Shut the Door After You

D—Protect Public Property

E—Replace the Newspapers After Reading

F—Round-the-clock Business

G—Seat by Number

H—See to the Fire

I—Shooting Prohibited

J—Stand Clear of the Power Line

K—Ticket Good only on the Day of Issue

L—Turn off the Light Before You Leave

M—Wet Paint

N—No Parking

O—Drive Slowly

P—Photographs：Please Don't Bend

Q—Children and Women First

R—For Use only in Case of Fire

S—Handle with Care

T—Keep Away From Fire

U—Keep Silence

V—Line up for Tickets

Examples：（K）当日有效   （J）高压电线　请勿靠近

51. (　　) 小心轻放   (　　) 禁止停车

52. (　　) 对号入座   (　　) 内有照片，请勿折叠

53. (　　) 昼夜营业   (　　) 不准转弯

54. (　　) 排队购票   (　　) 请随手关门

55. (　　) 油漆未干   (　　) 爱护公物

Task 5

Directions: *The following is a letter. After reading it, you are required to complete the statements that follow the questions (No. 56 to No. 60). You should write your answers in no more than 3 words on the corresponding Answer Sheet.*

Announcement

The swimming pool of Wuhan University will be open to the public on July 10 this year.

Time: 8:00 a.m.—8:00 p.m.

Fee: RMB 5 yuan / hr for an adult

　　　RMB 3 yuan / hr for a child

Please bring your own swimming suits.

---

56. When will the swimming pool begin to be open to the public?
    _____.

57. What time will the swimming pool close?
    _____.

58. How much will a grown-up pay if he stays in the swimming pool for 2 hours?
    _____.

59. How much will two children pay if they stay in the swimming pool for 3 hours?
    _____.

60. What do you need to bring when you go to the swimming pool?
    _____.

Part IV　Translation

Directions: *This part, numbered 61 through 65, is to test your ability to translate English into Chinese. After each of the sentences numbered 61 to 64, you will read four choices of suggested translation. You should choose the best translation and mark the corresponding letter on your Answer Sheet. And for the paragraph numbered 65, write your translation in the corresponding space on the Translation/ Composition Sheet.*

61. Hardly anyone can enjoy sitting in a train for more than a few hours.

　　A. 几乎没有人真的喜欢乘坐几个小时以上的火车。

　　B. 每个人都艰难地忍受乘坐几个小时以上的火车。

　　C. 有些人不喜欢乘坐几个小时以上的火车。

　　D. 很多人都以乘坐几个小时以上的火车为乐。

62. Which applicant do you think is more qualified for the job?

A. 你认为哪一位求职者更能胜任这份工作？
B. 你认为哪一位求职者合格？
C. 你认为哪一位适合这份工作？
D. 你认为他们做这份工作合适吗？

63. Her time is fully taken up with music.
    A. 音乐把她的时间都占领了。
    B. 她的时间都用于音乐了。
    C. 她把音乐填满了她的时间。
    D. 音乐把她的时间填满了。

64. He could not afford such a big house.
    A. 他不能承受这样的一个大房子。
    B. 他不可能承受这样的大房子。
    C. 他买不起这样的大房子。
    D. 他不可以买这样的大房子。

65. American love pets. Many pet owners treat their pets as members of the family. Sometimes they even buy entertaining videos and amusing toys for their pets. If they have an eye for fashion, pet owners can dress their pets in stylish clothes. On special occasions, they can use perfume to make their pets smell well. You might say Americans treat pets as they treat their children—sometimes even better.

Part V Writing

Directions: *This part is to test your ability to do practical writing. You are required to finish a congratulation letter to the following information given in Chinese. Remember to do the task on the Translation/Composition Sheet.*

1. 值此 2015 年即将到来之际，Tom 向 Mr. Barton 致以最良好的祝愿和问候。
2. 在新的一年里两国之间的文化交流，将有进一步的增加，并希望彼此之间的友好关系继续下去。

Unit 1

Part I Listening Comprehension

Section A

1-5: CBDAD

听力原稿

1. Excuse me, how far is the airport from here?
2. What's your hometown like, George?
3. Could you finish the paper today?
4. John, will you help me move this heavy box?
5. Tom, how about going to the theatre tonight?

Section B

6-10: BAACD

听力原稿

6. W: Hello, may I speak to Mr. Black?

   M: Sorry, he's not in at the moment. May I take a message?

   Q: What does the woman want to do?

7. M: May I have a look at that black jacket, please?

   W: Yes, what size do you take?

   Q: Where does this conversation most probably take place?

8. M: Excuse me, but when can I take the bus for the airport?

   W: There's a bus at 10 o'clock. You have to wait for five minutes.

   Q: What time is it now?

9. W: Professor Smith, here's the book you're looking for.

   M: Thanks. Where did you get it?

   Q: What does Professor Smith want?

10. M: What do you think of the new secretary?

W: Oh, she's a very nice person and she's quite young.

Q: How does the woman think the secretary is?

Section C

11. breakfast　　12. weather　　13. eight thirty　　14. saves　　15. fit

听力原稿

John is a bus driver. He gets up at six o'clock, eats a light breakfast in a hurry, and then rushes to work. He likes his job but hates to drive in bad weather. Rain and snow make the roads dangerous.

John's wife, Carol, works every day from eight thirty to noon as a bookkeeper. She likes keeping her house neat and tidy. She has a place for everything and throws out what she doesn't need. John is just the opposite. He saves everything. He keeps clothes that don't fit him any more, old magazines, boxes and papers. Nothing of his is in good order.

Part II　Vocabulary and Structure

Section A

16 – 20: DBCBA

21 – 25: BACBA

Section B

26. concerning　　27. rarity　　28. Pushy　　29. temptation　　30. recognition

31. prescription　　32. majority　　33. savings　　34. overdue　　35. idealistic

Part III　Reading Comprehension

36 – 40: CABDB

41 – 45: BACAC

46 – 50: BCADD

51. S, N　　52. G, P　　53. F, A　　54. V, C　　55. M, D

56. On July 10　　　　57. At 8:00p. m.　　　　58. RMB 10 yuan

59. RMB 18 yuan　　60. Swimming suits

Part IV　Translation

61 – 64: AABC

65. 美国人很爱宠物。很多宠物的主人把这些宠物当作家庭成员，有时候还为宠物购买娱乐用的录像带和有趣的玩具。如果宠物的主人喜欢赶时髦，还会让他们的宠物穿上时髦的衣服。特殊场合，他们甚至为宠物喷上专用香水，让它们的味道好闻一点。你也可以说，美国人对待他们的宠物如同对待他们的孩子一样——有时甚至更好。

Part V Writing

参考范文

Dear Mr. Barton:

  As the New Year is quickly approaching, I take this opportunity to send my greetings and best wishes to you for 2015.

  I hope that the coming year will bring a further increase in exchange of culture between our two countries and we look forward to continued friendly relations with you.

Yours faithfully,

Tom

Unit 2

Part I Listening Comprehension

Section A

Directions: *This section is to test your ability to understand short dialogues. There are 5 recorded dialogues in it. After each dialogue, there is a recorded question. Both the dialogues and questions will be spoken only once. When you hear a question, you should decide on the correct answer from the 4 choices marked A, B, C and D given in your test paper. Then you should mark the corresponding letter on the Answer Sheet with a single line through the center.*

1. A. I am very nice.   B. That's quite all right.   C. How do you do?   D. Thanks a lot.
2. A. In the morning.   B. Everyday.   C. In the classroom.   D. It's not important.
3. A. Yes, I do.   B. No, I don't.   C. No problem.   D. You are most welcome.
4. A. Let's work hard.   B. Thanks a lot.   C. You're welcome.   D. Tomorrow will be better.
5. A. The same to you. B. Not at all.   C. Glad to meet you. D. I am very happy.

Section B

Directions: *This section is to test your ability to understand short conversations. There are 5 recorded conversations in it. After each conversation, there is a recorded question. Both the conversations and questions will be spoken two times. When you hear a question, you should decide on the correct answer from the 4 choices marked A, B, C and D given in your test paper. Then you should mark the corresponding letter on the Answer Sheet with a single line through the center.*

6. A. She will pay for herself.   B. It will be better if the man pays for her.
    C. She will pay for the man.   D. She likes to have lunch in Dutch.
7. A. Her daughter's.   B. Her brother's.   C. Her sister's.   D. Her son's.
8. A. Manager and clerk.   B. Guest and waitress.
    C. Teacher and student.   D. Brother and sister.
9. A. 2 hours.   B. 2.5 hours.   C. 3 hours.   D. 3.5 hours.
10. A. The man's parents are very strict.   B. The man is not an adult.

C. She hates the man.   D. The man should adjust himself to college life.

Section C

Directions: *In this section you will hear a recorded short passage. The passage is printed on the test paper, but with some words or phrases missing. The passage will be read three times. During the second reading, you are required to put the missing words or phrases on the Answer Sheet in order of the numbered blanks according to what you hear. The third reading is for you to check your writing. Now the passage will begin.*

    I haven't seen you for a long time. How have you been? I am missing you 11_____ As the weather is splendid now, Jack, Lucy and I have made a plan to go out to the countryside by bike. Each of us may 12_____ for the picnic, which we will have at the hillside. The countryside must be very lovely, with grass and trees 13_____ heavily, flowers full bloom and bright sunshine. We can 14_____ the scenery to our hearts' content, at the same time and take some pictures as a memory. It is possible for us to meet at 15_____ at eight a.m. I am sure we will have a good time. Do come and join us.

11. _____
12. _____
13. _____
14. _____
15. _____

Part II Vocabulary and Structure

Directions: *This part is to test your ability to construct grammatically correct sentences. It consists of 2 sections.*

Section A

Directions: *In this section, there are 10 incomplete sentences. You are required to complete each one by deciding on the most appropriate word or words from the 4 choices marked A, B, C and D. Then you should mark the corresponding letter on the Answer Sheet with a single line through the center.*

16. —Hi, what did our monitor say just now?

    —Every boy and every girl as well as teachers who are to visit Water Cube _____ asked to be at the school gate before 6:30 in the morning.

    A. is   B. were   C. are   D. was

17. John as well as the other children who _____ no parents _____good care of in the center.

A. have; is being taken B. have; has taken
C. has; is taken D. has; have been taken

18. The number of people, who have access to their own cars, _____ sharply in the past decade.
    A. rose B. is rising C. have risen D. has risen
19. Professor Wang, together with his colleagues, _____ working on the project day and night to _____ the deadline.
    A. are; meet B. is; meet C. are; satisfy D. is; satisfy
20. Large quantities of information, as well as some timely help _____ since the organization was built.
    A. has offered B. had been offered C. have been offered D. is offered
21. The girl is so shy that she can't _____ very well _____ others.
    A. communicate; with
    B. communicate; to
    C. deal; with
    D. get along; to
22. It is obvious that hopes, goals, fear and desires _____ widely between men and women, between the rich and the poor.
    A. shift B. alter C. vary D. transfer
23. Mike _____ his parents to help him out of trouble.
    A. looked for B. dealt with C. turned to D. talked about
24. Whoever _____ in the robbery must be punished.
    A. involving B. involves C. involve D. is involved
25. The news _____ that Yao Ming would come to our school.
    A. grew B. carried C. developed D. spread

Section B

Directions: *There are 10 incomplete statements here. You should fill in each blank with the proper form of the word given in brackets. Write the word or words in the corresponding space on the Answer Sheet.*

26. His conduct is a mere cover-up for his _____ (nervous).
27. Once the price had been agreed, a deal was quickly _____ (conclude).
28. When asked to explain her behavior, she gave a very _____ (defend) answer.
29. There is a fine _____ (lay) of dust on the desk.
30. I _____ (lock) the door and went into the room.
31. I _____ (recognize) her the instant I saw her.
32. I met her quite by _____ (chance).
33. They are planning to _____ (construct) a new supermarket.

34. _____ (concentrate) is essential if you want to do a good job.

35. His _____ (treat) of her was beyond endurance.

Part Ⅲ Reading Comprehension

Directions: This part is to test your reading ability. There are 5 tasks for you to fulfill. You should read the reading materials carefully and do the tasks as you are instructed.

Task 1

Directions: After reading the following passage, you will find 5 questions or unfinished statements, numbered 36 to 40. For each question or statement there are 4 choices marked A, B, C and D. You should make the correct choice and mark the corresponding letter on the Answer Sheet with a single line through the center.

Fifteen years ago, I entered the Boston Globe, which was a temple to me then. It wasn't easy getting hired. But once you were there, I found, you were in.

Globe jobs were for life-guaranteed until retirement. For 15 years I had prospered there—moving from an ordinary reporter to foreign correspondent and finally to senior editor. I would have a lifetime of security if I stuck with it. Instead, I had made a decision to leave. I entered my boss's office. Would he rage? I wondered. He had a famous temper. "Matt, we have to have a talk," I began awkwardly. "I came to the Globe when I was twenty-four. Now I'm forty. There's a lot I want to do in life. I'm resigning." "To another paper?" he asked. I reached into my coat pocket, but didn't say anything. I handed him a letter that explained everything. It said that I was leaving to start a new media company. We were at a rare turning point in history. I wanted to be directly engaged in the change. "I'm glad for you," he said, quite out of my expectation. "I just came from a board of directors meeting and it was seventy-five percent discouraging news. Some of that we can deal with. But much of it we can't," he went on. "I wish you all the luck in the world," he concluded. "And if it doesn't work out, remember, your star is always high here."

Then I went out of his office, walking through the newsroom for more good-byes. Everybody was saying congratulations. Everybody—even though I'd be risking all on an unfamiliar venture: all the financial security I had carefully built up.

Later, I had a final talk with Bill Taylor, chairman and publisher of the Boston Globe. He had turned the Globe into a billion-dollar property. "I'm resigning, Bill," I said. He listened while I gave him the story. He wasn't looking angry or dismayed either. After a pause, he said, "Golly, I wish I were in your shoes."

36. From the passage we know that the Globe is a famous _____.

    A. newspaper   B. magazine   C. temple   D. church

37. If the writer stayed with the Globe _____.

A. he would be able to realize his lifetime dreams

B. he would let his long-cherished dreams fade away

C. he would never have to worry about his future life

D. he would never be allowed to develop his ambitions

38. The writer wanted to resign because _____.

    A. he had serious trouble with his boss

    B. he got underpaid at his job for the Globe

    C. he wanted to be engaged in the new media industry

    D. he had found a better paid job in a publishing house

39. When the writer decided to resign the Globe was faced with _____.

    A. a trouble with its staff members

    B. a shortage of qualified reporters

    C. an unfavorable business situation

    D. an uncontrollable business situation

40. By "I wish I were in your shoes." (in the last paragraph) Bill Taylor meant that _____.

    A. the writer was to fail

    B. the writer was stupid

    C. he would do the same if possible

    D. he would reject the writer's request

Task 2

Directions: *This task is the same as Task 1. The 5 questions or unfinished statements are numbered 41 to 45.*

During the hours when your labor through your work you may say that you're "hot." That's true. The time of day when you feel most energetic is when your cycle of body temperature is at its peak. For some people the peak comes during the forenoon. For others it comes in the afternoon or evening. No one has discovered why this is so, but it leads to such familiar monologues as: "Get up, Peter! You'll be late for work again!" The possible explanation to the trouble is that Peter is at his temperature-and-energy peak in the evening. Much family quarrelling ends when husbands and wives realize what these energy cycles mean, and which cycle each member of the family has.

You can't change your energy cycle, but you can learn to make your life fit it better. Habit can help, Dr. Kleitman believes. Maybe you're sleepy in the evening but feel you must stay up late anyway. Counteract your cycle to some extent by habitually staying up later than you want to. If your energy is low in the morning, but you have an important to do early in the day, rise before your usual hour. This won't change your cycle, but you'll get up steam and work better at your low point.

Get off to a slow start which saves your energy. Get up with a leisurely yawn and stretch. Sit on the edge of the bed a minute before putting your feet on the floor. Avoid the troublesome search for clean clothes by laying them out the night before. Whenever possible, do routine work in the afternoon and save requiring more energy or concentration for your sharper hours.

41. If a person finds getting up early a problem, most probably _____.

    A. he is a lazy person

    B. he refuses to follow his own energy cycle

    C. he is not sure when his energy is low

    D. he is at his peak in the afternoon or evening

42. Which of the following may lead to family quarrels according to the passage?

    A. Unawareness of energy cycles.

    B. Familiar monologues.

    C. A change in a family member's energy cycle.

    D. Attempts to control the energy cycle of other family members.

43. If one wants to work efficiently at his low point in the morning, he should _____.

    A. change his energy cycle

    B. overcome his laziness

    C. get up earlier than usual

    D. go to bed earlier

44. You are advised to rise with a yawn and stretch because it will _____.

    A. help to keep your energy for the day's work

    B. help you to control your temper early in the day

    C. enable you to concentrate on your routine work

    D. keep your energy cycle under control all day

45. Which of the following statements is NOT true?

    A. Getting off to work with a minimum effort helps save one's energy.

    B. Dr. Kletman explains why people reach their peaks at different hours of day.

    C. Habit helps a person adapt to his own energy cycle.

    D. Children have energy cycles, too.

Task 3

Directions: *After reading the following passage, you will find 5 questions or unfinished statements, numbered 46 to 50. For each question or statement there are 4 choices marked A, B, C and D. You should make the correct choice and mark the corresponding letter on the Answer Sheet with a single line through the center.*

There was one thought that air pollution affected only the area immediately around large cities with factories and heavy automobile traffic. At present, we realize that although these are the areas with the worst air pollution, the problem is literally worldwide. On several occasions over the past decade, a heavy cloud of air pollution has covered the east of the United States and brought health warnings in rural areas away from any major concentration of manufacturing and automobile traffic. In fact, the very climate of the entire earth may be infected by air pollution. Some scientists consider that the increasing concentration of carbon dioxide in the air resulting from the burning of fossil fuels (coal and oil) is creating a "greenhouse effect" — conserving heat reflected from the earth and raising the world's average temperature. If this view is correct and the world's temperature is raised only a few degrees, much of the polar ice cap will melt and cities such as New York, Boston, Miami, and New Orleans will be in water.

Another view, less widely held, is that increasing particular matter in the atmosphere is blocking sunlight and lowering the earth's temperature—a result that would be equally disastrous. A drop of just a few degrees could create something close to a new ice age, and would make agriculture difficult or impossible in many of our top farming areas. Today we do not know for sure that either of these conditions will happen (though one recent government report drafted by experts in the field concluded that the greenhouse effect is very possible). Perhaps, if we are lucky enough, the two tendencies will offset each other and the world's temperature will stay about the same as it is now. Driven by economic profits, people neglect the damage on our environment caused by the "advanced civilization." Maybe the air pollution is the price the human beings have to pay for their development. But is it really worthwhile?

46. As pointed out at the beginning of the passage, people used to think that air pollution _____.
    A. caused widespread damage in the countryside
    B. affected the entire eastern half of the United States
    C. had damaged effect on health
    D. existed merely in urban and industries areas
47. As to the greenhouse effect, the author _____.
    A. shares the same view with the scientist
    B. is uncertain of its occurrence
    C. rejects it as being ungrounded
    D. thinks that it will destroy the world soon
48. The word "offset" in the second paragraph could be replaced by _____.
    A. slip into   B. make up for   C. set up   D. catch up with
49. It can be concluded that _____.
    A. raising the world's temperature only a few degrees would not do much harm to life on earth
    B. lowering the world's temperature merely a few degrees would lead major farming areas to disaster

C. almost no temperature variations have occurred over the past decade

D. the world's temperature will remain constant in the years to come

50. This passage is primarily about _____.

A. the greenhouse effect

B. the burning of fossil fuels

C. the potential effect of air pollution

D. the likelihood of a new ice age

Task 4

Directions: *Read the following article in which five people talk about their ideas of dieting. For questions 51 to 55, match name of each speaker to one of the statements (A to G) given below. Mark your answers on your ANSWER SHEET.*

Abbey

You can always recognize dieters from the sour expression on their faces. They spend most of their time turning their noses up at food. They are forever consulting calorie charts, gazing at themselves in mirrors, and leaping on to weighing-machines in the bathroom. They spend a lifetime fighting a losing battle against spreading hips, protruding tummies and double chins. What a miserable lot dieters are!

Marlin

I began making some dietary and lifestyles changes during my second year of college and have been eating this way ever since. I like the way I feel when I don't eat animal foods so much more than the pleasure I used to get from eating them. I have much more energy; I need less sleep; I feel calmer; I can maintain an ideal body weight without worrying about how much I eat, and I can think more clearly.

Maggie

During my first year of college, I gained forty pounds when I began throwing the javelin. For the next twenty years, I carried all of this extra weight and kidded myself that I was in good shape since that's what I weighed in college. Now that I've lost all that extra weight, I feel great! People say all the time, "Well, how do you live without eating cheeseburgers or this or that?" and I say, "You just don't. It's not even an option. It's not that hard once you get on it."

Belinda

If you are on a diet, you're always hungry. You can't be hungry and happy at the same time. All the horrible concoctions you eat instead of food leave you permanently dissatisfied. A complete food it may be, but not quite as complete as juicy steak. So at least three times a day you will be exposed to temptation. How miserable to watch others tucking into piles of mouth-watering food while you munch a water biscuit and sip unsweetened lemon juice! And if hunger just proves too much for you, in the end you will lash out and devour five huge guilt-inducing cream cakes at a sitting. Then things will turn out to be even worse.

Wood

I went on diet when my doctor told me that my blood pressure tended to be high. Only at that time did I realize the danger of being overweight. Since I began making dietary changes in 1982, eating this way has become increasingly accepted. I don't feel I've lost something after dieting. Instead, I've got something valuable. That is good health.

Now match each of the persons to the appropriate statement.

Note: there are two extra statements.

Names   Statements
51. Abbey   A. Being on a diet is a torture.
52. Marlin   B. I feel better with vegetarian food.
53. Maggie   C. I lost weight after dieting.
54. Belinda   D. I began dieting for the sake of health.
55. Wood   E. Dieting enables people to enjoy life more.
                        F. Dieting simply causes endless worries.
                        G. Dieting does more harm than good to one's health.

Task 5

Directions: *The following is a list of terms related to professions. After reading it, you are required to find the items equivalent to (与……等同) those given in Chinese in the table below. Then you should put the corresponding letters in brackets on the Answer Sheet, numbered 51 through 55.*

A—CEO   B—Administrative Assistant
C—Assistant Manager   D—Buyer
E—Cashier   F—Lawyer
G—Clerk/Receptionist   H—Computer Engineer
I—Deputy General Manager   J—Engineering Technician
K—Tour Guide   L—Photographer
M—General Manager Assistant   N—Sales Manager
O—Journalist / Reporter

Examples: (I) 副总经理   (D) 采购员
56. (   ) 销售经理   (   ) 计算机工程师
57. (   ) 记者   (   ) 总经理助理
58. (   ) 律师   (   ) 导游
59. (   ) 职员/接待员   (   ) 摄影师
60. (   ) 工程技术员   (   ) 总裁

Part IV Translation

Directions: *This part, numbered 61 through 65, is to test your ability to translate English into Chinese. After each of the sentences numbered 61 to 64, you will read four choices of suggested translation. You should choose the best translation and mark the corresponding letter on your Answer Sheet. And for the paragraph numbered 65, write your translation in the corresponding space on the Translation/ Composition Sheet.*

61. If you work with great application in your studies, you will succeed.

    A. 如果在学习中你有所应用，你就能成功。

    B. 如果你学习刻苦勤奋，你就会成功。

    C. 你如果提出申请学习，你会得到批准。

    D. 如果你在学习中表现努力，你会成功。

62. My income is now twice as much as I used to earn two years ago.

    A. 我两年前的收入是现在的两倍。

    B. 我现在的收入是两年前的两倍。

    C. 我两年前的收入比现在高两倍。

    D. 我现在的收入比两年前高两倍。

63. It is in our best interest to make it easier for them to engage in their own internal negotiations.

    A. 让他们容易参加内部谈判是我们的最大兴趣。

    B. 让他们容易从事内部协商事务是我们的最大兴趣。

    C. 让他们能较为轻松地进行内部谈判符合我们的最大利益。

    D. 让他们能较为轻松地从事内部协商事务符合我们的最大利益。

64. Part-time work is sometimes a matter of choice, sometimes a matter of necessity.

    A. 兼职工作有时是出于个人选择，有时则是出于必要。

    B. 兼职工作有时是供你选择，有时则是必须选择。

    C. 兼职工作有时是有许多工种，有时则是没得选必须做。

    D. 兼职工作有时指选择做的事情，有时则是指必须要做的事情。

65. On behalf of our company, I would like to say how delighted we are to receive you here in Shanghai. It's been a great pleasure to have the presence of the general manager and his delegation here tonight. I hope that through our joint efforts, the future trade between us will expand even further.

Part V Writing

Directions: *This part is to test your ability to do practical writing. You are required to complete the letter according to the following information given in Chinese. Remember to do the task on the Translation/Composition Sheet.*

  某校一位教师邀请你去给学生们做有关在国外进行长期投资的讲座,你对邀请表示感谢,并表示乐意参加,同时还商定好了讲座的时间和地点。你还指出希望能把你信中附寄的有关你公司在全球投资情况的小册子先发给学生看,以帮助学生们更好地了解这方面的知识。

Unit 2

Part I Listening Comprehension

Section A

1-5: CBCBA

听力原稿

1. How do you do?
2. How often do you study English?
3. Can you do me a favor?
4. Wish you every success in the coming year!
5. Merry Christmas!

Section B

6-10: ADCCD

听力原稿

6. M: Will you have lunch with me?

    W: Yes, but let's go Dutch.

    Q: What does the woman mean?

7. M: Let's congratulate you on the birth of your son.

    W: Thank you. I hope he will grow up happily.

    Q: Whose birth is it?

8. M: Please do remember to hand in your essay tomorrow morning.

    W: Oh, my God. How can I finish it within a few hours?

    Q: What's the probable relationship between the two speakers?

9. M: What are you planning to do this evening?

    W: Well. I plan to study English for one hour, Chinese for half an hour, and Mathematics for one hour and a half.

    Q: How long does the woman plan to study?

10. M: I'm not quite used to college life. Sometimes I really want to go back home.
   W: Don't be foolish. You are an adult now.
   Q: What does the woman mean?

Section C

11. all the time   12. take food   13. growing   14. enjoy   15. the bus stop

听力原稿

　　I haven't seen you for a long time. How have you been? I am missing you all the time. As the weather is splendid now, Jack, Lucy and I have made a plan to go out to the countryside by bike. Each of us may take food for the picnic, which we will have at the hillside. The countryside must be very lovely, with grass and trees growing heavily, flowers full bloom and bright sunshine. We can enjoy the scenery to our hearts'content, at the same time and take some pictures as a memory. It is possible for us to meet at the bus stop at eight a. m. I am sure we will have a good time. Do come and join us.

Part II Vocabulary and Structure

Section A

16－20: AADBC
21－25: ACCDD

Section B

26. nervousness   27. concluded   28. defensive   29. layer   30. unlocked
31. recognized   32. chance   33. construct   34. Concentration   35. treatment

Part III Reading Comprehension

36－40: ACCCC
41－45: DACAB
46－50: DBBBC
51－55: ABCGD
56. N, H   57. O, M   58. F, K   59. G, L   60. J, A

Part IV Translation

61－64   BBCA

65. 我代表公司非常高兴地在上海接待你们。总经理及其代表团成员今晚的光临让我们感到非常荣幸。我希望通过我们的共同努力,将来我们之间的贸易会进一步扩大。

Part V Writing

参考范文

19 June 2008

Dear Mr. Liu of Jiang Xi University,

   This is to acknowledge receipt of your invitation letter of 20 May 2008, and your invitation to ask me to offer students of your university a lecture about long term investment abroad has been accepted with pleasure. I agree the timing and place of the lecture you indicated in your letter. If you can arrange some transportation to pick me up by the time, it will be very convenient to me.

   Enclosed please find the catalogues I would like to show your students before the lecture takes place so that they can have a full knowledge on the situation of our company's investments worldwide.

   Thank you again for the opportunity and I am looking forward to seeing you soon.

Sincerely yours,
× ×

Encl. 3 catalogues

Unit 3

Part I Listening Comprehension

Directions: *This part is to test your listening ability. It consists of 3 sections.*

Section A

Directions: *This section is to test your ability to understand short dialogues. There are 5 recorded dialogues in it. After each dialogue, there is a recorded question. Both the dialogues and questions will be spoken only once. When you hear a question, you should decide on the correct answer from the 4 choices marked A, B, C and D given in your test paper. Then you should mark the corresponding letter on the Answer Sheet with a single line through the center.*

1. A. A teacher. B. A doctor.
   C. A secretary. D. A salesman.
2. A. Visiting a company. B. Meeting with the new manager.
   C. Looking for the meeting room. D. Showing a newcomer around.
3. A. In an office. B. In a restaurant.
   C. In a department store. D. In a library.
4. A. To attend a conference. B. To work in a firm.
   C. To do some sightseeing. D. To visit an exhibition.
5. A. The rise of costs. B. The drop of sales.
   C. The decrease of production. D. The increase of pollution.

Section B

Directions: *This section is to test your ability to understand short conversations. There are 2 recorded conversations in it. After each conversation, there are some recorded questions. Both the conversations and questions will be spoken two times. When you hear a question, you should decide on the correct answer from the 4 choices marked A, B, C and D given in your test paper. Then you should mark the corresponding letter on the Answer Sheet with a single line through the center.*

Conversation 1

6. A. All staff. B. Young workers.
   C. New employees. D. Department manager.
7. A. 1 week. B. 2 weeks.
   C. 3 weeks. D. 4 weeks.
8. A. How to operate machines. B. How to use computers.
   C. How to collect information. D. How to be a manager.

Conversation 2

9. A. Because there was no access to the Internet.
   B. Because the traffic outside was too noisy.
   C. Because the air conditioner was out of order.
   D. Because there was no hot water in the bath.
10. A. Room 201. B. Room 203.
    C. Room 204. D. Room 206.

Section C

Directions: *This section is to test your ability to comprehend short passages. You will hear a recorded passage. After that you will hear five questions. Both the passage and the questions will be read two times. When you hear a question, you should complete the answer to it with a word or a short phrase (in no more than 3 words). The questions and incomplete answers are printed in your test paper. You should write your answers on the Answer Sheet correspondingly. Now listen to the passage.*

11. What's Peter Johnson's position in the company?
    He is the _____ Manager.
12. What places will the visitors see in the company?
    _____ and the laboratory.
13. How long does it take to look around the laboratory?
    About _____ minutes.
14. What measures are taken to ensure the visitors' safety?
    The visitors are required to wear protective hard hats and _____.
15. What is not allowed to do during the tour?
    _____.

Part Ⅱ Vocabulary and Structure

Directions: *This part is to test your ability to construct grammatically correct sentences. It consists of 2 sections.*

Section A

Directions: *In this section, there are 10 incomplete sentences. You are required to complete each one by deciding on the most appropriate word or words from the 4 choices marked A, B, C and D. Then you should mark the corresponding letter on the Answer Sheet with a single line through the center.*

16. We must find a way to cut prices _____ reducing our profits too much.
    A. without   B. despite   C. with   D. for
17. She didn't know _____ to express her ideas in English clearly in public.
    A. which   B. why   C. what   D. how
18. _____ the weather improves, we will suffer a huge loss in the tourist industry.
    A. As   B. Since   C. While   D. Unless
19. We are happy at the good news _____ Mr. Black has been awarded the Best Manager.
    A. that   B. which   C. what   D. whether
20. It is important that we _____ the task ahead of time.
    A. will finish   B. finished   C. finish   D. shall finish
21. Would you please pass me the book _____ cover is black?
    A. which   B. whose   C. that   D. its
22. _____ in the company for three years, Mark has become experienced in business negotiations.
    A. Having worked   B. Have been working
    C. Have worked   D. Worked
23. Not until she arrived at the meeting room _____ she had forgotten to bring the document.
    A. she realized   B. did she realize   C. she did realize   D. does she realize
24. John had never been abroad before, _____ he found the business trip very exciting.
    A. because   B. though   C. so   D. while
25. _____ some students are able to find employment after graduation, others will have to return to school and earn an advanced degree.
    A. Since   B. While   C. Because   D. If

Section B

Directions: *There are 10 incomplete statements here. You should fill in each blank with the proper form of the word given in brackets. Write the word or words in the corresponding space on the Answer Sheet.*

26. Employees are not allowed (make) _____ personal phone calls in the office.
27. The shop assistant priced the goods before (put) _____ them on the shelf.
28. The purpose of new technology is to make life (easy) _____, not to make it more diffi-

cult.

29. The proposal about the annual sales (discuss) _____ at the next board meeting.
30. Since we work in different sections of the company, we see each other only (occasional) _____.
31. Some domestic manufacturers are busy increasing production, losing the chance to develop more (advance) _____ technology.
32. I shall appreciate your effort in (correct) _____ this error in my bank account as soon as possible.
33. If your neighbors are too noisy, then you have a good reason to make your (complain) _____.
34. 30 percent of the students who (interview) _____ yesterday believe they should continue with their education until they have a university degree.
35. Measures should be taken to avoid the negative effect (bring) _____ about by unfair competition.

Part III Reading Comprehension

Directions: *This part is to test your reading ability. There are 5 tasks for you to fulfill. You should read the reading materials carefully and do the tasks as you are instructed.*

Task 1

Directions: *After reading the following passage, you will find 5 questions or unfinished statements, numbered 36 to 40. For each question or statement there are 4 choices marked A, B, C and D. You should make the correct choice and mark the corresponding letter on the Answer Sheet with a single line through the center.*

Google, the Internet search-engine company, has announced it will give more than twenty-five million dollars in money and investments to help the poor. The company says the effort involves using the power of information and technology to help people improve their lives.

Aleem Walji works for Google. org—the part of the company that gives money to good causes. He said the company's first project will help identify where infectious (传染性的) diseases are developing. In Southeast Asia and Africa, for example, Google. org will work with partners to strengthen early-warning systems and take action against growing health threats.

Google. org's second project will invest in ways to help small and medium-sized businesses grow. Walji says microfinance (小额信贷) is generally small, short-term loans that create few jobs. Instead, he says Google. org wants to develop ways to bring investors and business owners together to create jobs and improve economic growth.

Google. org will also give money to help two climate-change programs announced earlier this year. One of these programs studies ways to make renewable (再生的) energy less costly than coal-based energy. The other is examining the efforts being made to increase the use of electric cars.

The creators of Google have promised to give Google. org about one percent of company profits and one percent of its total stock value every year. Aleem Walji says this amount may increase in the future.

36. The purpose of Google's investments is to _____.
    A. help poor people
    B. develop new technology
    C. expand its own business
    D. increase the power of information

37. According to Aleem Walji, the company's first project is to _____.
    A. set up a new system to warn people of infectious diseases
    B. find out where infectious diseases develop
    C. identify the causes of infectious diseases
    D. cure patients of infectious diseases

38. What kind of businesses will benefit from Google. org's second project?
    A. Large enterprises.
    B. Cross-national companies.
    C. Foreign-funded corporations.
    D. Small and medium-sized businesses.

39. From the fourth paragraph, we learn that Google's money is also invested to help _____.
    A. start more research programs
    B. make more advanced electric cars
    C. develop renewable and coal-based energy
    D. conduct studies related to climate changes

40. From the last paragraph we learn that the investments by Google. org come from _____.
    A. Google's profits and stock value
    B. some international IT companies
    C. the company's own interests
    D. local commercial banks

Task 2

Directions: *This task is the same as Task 1. The 5 questions or unfinished statements are numbered 41 to 45.*

Your boss holds your future prospects in his hands. Some bosses are hard to get along with. Some have excellent qualifications but no idea when it comes to dealing with people. Of course, not all bosses are like that.

The relationship you have with your boss can be a major factor in determining your rise up the career ladder. Your boss is not only your leader, he is also the person best equipped to help you do the job you are paid to do. He can inform you of company direction that may affect your professional development.

Your boss also needs you to perform at your best in order to accomplish his objectives. He needs your feedback in order to provide realistic and useful reports to upper management. But how does this help you establish a meaningful working relationship with your boss?

The key is communication. Learn and understand his goals and priorities (优先的事). Observe and understand your boss's work style. If he has not been clear with his expectations, ask! Likewise, ask for feedback and accept criticism gracefully. And if he understands that you do not view your job as just something to fill the hours between 9 and 5, he may be more likely to help you.

In short, getting along with your boss requires getting to know his likes and dislikes and learning to work with his personality and management style.

41. The main idea of the first paragraph is that _____.
    A. bosses are hard to deal with   B. bosses have good character
    C. bosses determine your career future D. bosses must have similar personality

42. In the second paragraph, "rise up the career ladder" (Line 2) means _____.
    A. going to work abroad   B. changing jobs frequently
    C. being promoted in position   D. pursuing an advanced degree

43. In order to achieve his objectives, your boss expects that you will _____.
    A. do your best in your work   B. show your management skills
    C. get along with your colleagues   D. write reports to upper management

44. The most important factor for establishing a good working relationship with the boss is _____.
    A. high expectations   B. quick feedback
    C. frequent criticism   D. effective communication

45. The best title for the passage might be _____.
    A. How to Take Care of Your Boss   B. How to Get Along with Your Boss
    C. How to Accept Your Boss's Criticism D. How to Accomplish Your Boss's Objective

Task 3

Directions: *The following is an announcement. After reading it, you are required to complete the outline below it (No. 46 to No. 50). You should write your answers briefly (in no more than three words) on the Answer Sheet correspondingly.*

We welcome you aboard the Eastern Flight and will do our best to make your trip comfortable and enjoyable.

For your safety and convenience

To begin the trip, we would like to draw your attention to some safety-related details. These are also explained on the instruction card in the seat pocket in front of you. Seat belts must remain fastened while the "Fasten seatbelts" sign is on. It is advisable to keep them fastened at all times while seated. All flights are non-smoking. The use of mobile telephones is now allowed when the airplane is on the ground. During the flight the use of CD and DVD players is not allowed.

For your entertainment

To help you enjoy your trip, we provide a range of newspapers. On our MD – 11 and Boeing aircraft, we provide music and video programs. On Airbus A 321/320/319, short videos are shown.

Meals and drinks

During most flights we serve you a tasty meal and drinks. Beer, wine and other drinks are served free of charge. Coffee, tea and juice are served free of charge on all domestic (国内的) flights. On domestic flights leaving before nine and on all flights to Northern China, a snack is served.

Eastern Flight Service

Safety and convenience

1) Seat belts: remain __46__ while the "Fasten seatbelts" sign is on

2) Smoking: not allowed on board

3) Mobile phones: used only when the airplane is __47__

4) CD and DVD: not allowed to play __48__

Entertainment provided

1) newspapers

2) music and __49__ on MD – 11 and Boeing aircraft

Meals and drinks on board

1) meals served on most flights

2) coffee, tea and juice served free of charge

3) a snack served on all flights to __50__

Task 4

Directions: *The following is a list of terms related to Security. After reading it, you are required to find the items equivalent to (与……等同) those given in Chinese in the table below. Then you should put the corresponding letters in the brackets on the Answer Sheet, numbered 51 through 55.*

A—air traffic control system   B—armed police

C—crime prevention   D—entry requirement

E—international criminal police organization

F—level of security   G—picket line

H—police station   I—patrolling vehicle

J—safety precaution measure   K—safety control device

L—security command center   M—security service

N—security control center   O—security personnel

P—valid documents   Q—security monitoring and control

Examples: (M) 保安服务　　　　　(G) 警戒线
51. (　　) 空中交通管制系统　　(　　) 安全预防措施
52. (　　) 巡逻车　　　　　　　(　　) 武装警察
53. (　　) 国际刑警组织　　　　(　　) 有效证件
54. (　　) 入境要求　　　　　　(　　) 安保人员
55. (　　) 安全保障级别　　　　(　　) 安全监控

Task 5

Directions: *The following is a business letter. After reading it, you should give brief answers to the 5 questions (No. 56 to No. 60) that follow. The answers (in no more than 3 words) should be written after the corresponding numbers on the Answer Sheet.*

Dear Mr. Smith,

I am pleased to offer you the position of after-sales manager at our company starting on 16 June, 2009. I propose that the terms of employment will be those in the attached draft individual employment agreement.

Please note that you are entitled to discuss this offer and to seek advice on the attached proposed agreement with your family, a union, a lawyer, or someone else you trust. If you want some information on your employment rights, you can also contact the Employment Service Office or visit our website.

Also, if you disagree with, or do not understand or wish to clarify anything in this offer, please ring me to discuss any issue you wish to raise.

If you are happy with the proposed terms and wish to accept this offer of employment, please sign the duplicate copy of this letter and return it to me by 1 June, 2009. In the event I have not heard from you by that date, this offer will be automatically withdrawn on that date.

I look forward to working with you.

Yours sincerely,

John Brown

56. What job position is offered to Mr. Smith in the letter?
    _____.

57. From whom may Mr. Smith seek advice about the proposed agreement?
    His family, a union, _____, or someone else he trusts.

58. How can Mr. Smith get information about employment rights?
    By contacting the _____ or visiting its website.

59. When should Mr. Smith return the signed duplicate copy of this letter?
    By _____.

60. What will happen if the duplicate copy of the letter is not returned by the deadline?

This offer will be _____ on that date.

Part IV Translation

Directions: *This part, numbered 61 through 65, is to test your ability to translate English into Chinese. After each of the sentences numbered 61 to 64, you will read four choices of suggested translation. You should choose the best translation and mark the corresponding letter on your Answer Sheet. And for the paragraph numbered 65, write your translation in the corresponding space on the Translation/ Composition Sheet.*

61. If either party wants to renew the contract, it should submit a written notice to the other party three months prior to the expiration of the contract.

    A. 如果任何一方希望撤销合约，必须将撤销的理由在三个月内通知对方。
    B. 如果合同一方希望重签合同，必须在合同到期三个月内写信通知对方。
    C. 如果任何一方希望更改合同，必须提前三个月向对方书面提交其理由。
    D. 如果合同一方希望续签合同，必须在合同期满前三个月书面通知对方。

62. There is no sign that the world economic crisis will lessen in the next few months, although a certain degree of recovery is in sight.

    A. 尽管没有人认为未来几个月内世界经济危机会消失，但是在一定程度上的复苏是肯定的。
    B. 尽管世界经济复苏的迹象是肯定的，但是未来几个月内经济危机缓和的现象还不很明显。
    C. 尽管已经显现出一定程度的经济复苏，但没有迹象表明世界经济危机在未来几个月会减缓。
    D. 尽管没有人承认未来几个月内世界经济危机会触底，但我们肯定会看到世界经济的复苏。

63. Most of the issues concerning personnel management have been solved satisfactorily; only a few of secondary importance remain to be discussed.

    A. 多数有关人员管理的问题顺利地解决了，仅剩下几个问题还需要进行第二次讨论。
    B. 大多数有关人事管理问题已经得到圆满解决，只剩下几个次要的问题还有待于讨论。
    C. 很多有关人员配备问题基本上都得到了答复，只有第二个重要问题还未经过讨论。
    D. 第二个重要问题是有关人员调动的问题，这次已经得到妥善解决，不必再次讨论。

64. Only in this way can Chinese enterprises improve their competitiveness and avoid being defeated by their foreign rivals after China's entry into the WTO.

    A. 只有这个方法才能帮助中国企业去参加竞争，避免在加入世贸组织后被其外国对手所击败。
    B. 只有这样中国企业才能提高竞争力，并且在中国加入世贸组织后不会败给他们的外国对手。

C. 如果中国企业要想在世贸组织中参加竞争，必须通过这种办法才能击败他们的外国对手。

D. 中国企业只有通过这种途径来击败外国的对手，才能表明他们在世贸组织中具备竞争力。

65. Thank you, Mr. Black. It's a great honor to be appointed as Overseas Sales Manager. To be honest, this promotion came as quite a surprise to me. I'd like to think it's mainly the contribution of the whole team. I'd like to thank all my colleagues in the company for their support and hard work. Due to their efforts, we've started some overseas projects successfully. Looking to the future, I'd still like to maintain contact with everyone, even though I'll be working at the management level.

Part V Writing

说明：根据下面中文信息写一封询问信。

发信人：Mark Zhang

收信人：Mr. Smith

发信日期：2009 年 12 月 22 日

内容：

1. Mark 在最近的广交会上认识了 Smith 先生；

2. Mark 对 Smith 先生所在公司展出的新款手机很感兴趣；

3. 询问产品的详细信息，包括产品的规格、颜色、价格和功能等；

4. 说明看好该款手机市场销售前景；

5. 希望和对方建立长远的商务关系。

Words for references:

广交会 Guangzhou Trade Fair

规格 specifications

Unit 3

Part I Listening Comprehension

Section A

1-5: DCBAB

听力原稿

1. W: What's your present job, please?

   M: I'm a salesman. I work with a trade company.

   Q: What is the man's job?

2. M: Excuse me, I'm a newcomer here. Where is the meeting room?

   W: Oh, it's on the second floor.

   Q: What's the man doing now?

3. W: Are we ready to order, Sir?

   M: Well, sandwich, some food, salad, and a cup of coffee.

   Q: Where are the two speakers?

4. W: Mr. Smith, is this your first visit to China?

   M: Yes, I'm here for the international conference.

   Q: Why has the man come to China?

5. M: Jay, what're you worried about?

   W: Well, the sales of the company dropped again this month.

   Q: What is the company's problem?

Section B

6-10: CCABD

听力原稿

Conversation 1

M: Hi, Betty, may I have a discussion about the training program with you?

W: Sure. Take a seat, please.

M: We are planning a training program for the new employees. They have to learn how to use the machines.

W: That's fine. How about the training time?

M: Normally it takes three weeks.

W: At present, almost all operations are controlled by computers. I think two-weeks training will be enough.

M: But some employees know nothing about the computer.

W: In that case, let's make it three weeks.

M: OK, thank you.

Q6: Who will be trained in the program?

Q7: How long will the training program last?

Q8: What is the training program mainly about?

Conversation 2

M: Excuse me, I would like to change rooms if possible.

W: Sure. But could you tell me why?

M: The traffic outside is too noisy. I couldn't sleep at all last night.

W: I'm sorry to hear that Sir. Let me check and see what is available.

M: Thank you.

W: Well, we have a few rooms available.

M: Great, can I change my room right now?

W: Which room are you in?

M: Room 201.

W: Can I put you into Room 206, on the opposite side, away from the street?

M: OK, what do I need to do to transfer?

W: Let me check you out of your old room first.

Q9: Why does the man want to change his room?

Q10: Which room will the man move to?

Section C

11. Production   12. The factory   13. 10 / ten   14. safety glasses   15. Smoking

听力原稿

Ladies and gentlemen, welcome to the company. My name is Peter Johnson. I'm the Production Manager. I'll be showing you around today. It should take about twenty minutes to see the factory, and another ten minutes to take a look at the laboratory. Altogether our tour should last about half an hour. During the tour, please feel free to ask questions. I'll be happy to answer them. Now please wear these protective hard hats and safety glasses! Because we must care about your safety and we want to ensure there're no injuries. I must also tell you that smoking is not allowed during the tour. Well, if you don't have any questions, shall we get started? First, I'll take you to the factory. This way, please.

Q11: What's Peter Johnson's position in the company?
Q12: What places will the visitors see in the company?
Q13: How long does it take to look around the laboratory?
Q14: What measures are taken to ensure the visitors' safety?
Q15: What is not allowed to do during the tour?

Part Ⅱ   Vocabulary and Structure

Section A

16-20: ADDAC
21-25: BABCB

Section B

26. to make   27. putting   28. easier
29. will be discussed / is to be discussed / should be discussed
30. occasionally   31. advanced   32. correcting
33. complaint   34. were interviewed   35. brought

Part Ⅲ   Reading Comprehension

36-40: ABDDA
41-45: CCADB
46. fastened   47. on the ground   48. during the flight
49. video programs   50. Northern China
51. A, J 52. I, B 53. E, P 54. D, O 55. F, Q
56. (The) after-sales manager   57. a lawyer   58. Employment Service Office
59. 1 June, 2009   60. (automatically) withdrawn

Part Ⅳ   Translation

61-64: DCBB
65. 谢谢您，布莱克先生。被任命为海外销售部经理，我感到极大的荣幸。坦白说，这次升迁令我十分意外。我想这主要是整个团队的功劳。我要感谢公司全体同人们的支持与努力。

由于他们的努力，我们海外的一些项目已经顺利地启动了。展望未来，尽管我将在管理层工作，我仍希望与大家保持联系。

Part V Writing

参考范文

Dear Mr. Smith,

  I'm Mark Zhang. I met you for the first time during Guangzhou Trade Fair recently, and I'm interested in your new mobile. Could you please give me some information about the new product that produced by your firm?

  Please tell me the specifications as well as the color about the mobile. Also I hope you can tell something about the price and functions. I'm confident in the market situation of your new product.

  I hope we can have a nice and lasting cooperation.

Yours sincerely
Zhang

Unit 4

Part I Listening Comprehension

Directions: *This part is to test your listening ability. It consists of 3 sections.*

Section A

Directions: *This section is to test your ability to understand short dialogues. There are 5 recorded dialogues in it. After each dialogue, there is a recorded question. Both the dialogues and questions will be spoken only once. When you hear a question, you should decide on the correct answer from the 4 choices marked A, B, C and D given in your test paper. Then you should mark the corresponding letter on the Answer Sheet with a single line through the center.*

1. A. In the hotel.   B. In Henry Bellow's room.
   C. At the airport.   D. In the restaurant.
2. A. At 10:30.   B. At 10:25.
   C. At 10:40.   D. At 10:45.
3. A. Go to the library.   B. Meet the woman.
   C. See Professor Smith.   D. Go to the class.
4. A. Jane often comes late for her class.   B. Jane is a new comer.
   C. Jane had nothing to do this morning.   D. Jane went to bed late last night.
5. A. The semester.   B. College life.
   C. English Club.   D. A member.

Section B

Directions: *This section is to test your ability to understand short conversations. There are 2 recorded conversations in it. After each conversation, there are some recorded questions. Both the conversations and questions will be spoken two times. When you hear a question, you should decide on the correct answer from the 4 choices marked A, B, C and D given in your test paper. Then you should mark the corresponding letter on the Answer Sheet with a single line through the center.*

Conversation 1

6. A. Customer and salesgirl.　　B. Customer and waitress.
   C. Husband and wife.　　D. Employee and boss.
7. A. More expensive.　　B. Cheaper.
   C. The same as the tickets upstairs.　　D. Four pounds.
8. A. Show the film.　　B. Listen to the music.
   C. Talk about the film.　　D. Go to the cinema.

Conversation 2

9. A. In the factory.　　B. In the shop.
   C. At the Trade Fair.　　D. In the US.
10. A. 20, 000.　　B. 200, 000.
    C. 10, 000.　　D. 100, 000.

Section C

Directions: *This section is to test your ability to comprehend short passages. You will hear a recorded passage. After that you will hear five questions. Both the passage and the questions will be read two times. When you hear a question, you should complete the answer to it with a word or a short phrase (in no more than 3 words). The questions and incomplete answers are printed in your test paper. You should write your answers on the Answer Sheet correspondingly. Now listen to the passage.*

11. The Port of Shanghai faces _____.
12. Shanghai is the country's largest _____ center.
13. Access to various parts of the country is provided by _____ and inland navigation.
14. Its annual cargo handling has reached _____.
15. To accomplish _____.

Part II　Vocabulary and Structure

Directions: *This part is to test your ability to construct grammatically correct sentences. It consists of 2 sections.*

Section A

Directions: *In this section, there are 10 incomplete sentences. You are required to complete each one by deciding on the most appropriate word or words from the 4 choices marked A, B, C and D. Then you should mark the corresponding letter on the Answer Sheet with a single line through the center.*

16. —I haven't heard from Henry for a long time.
    — What do you suppose _____ to him?

A. was happening   B. to happen   C. has happened   D. had happened

17. No one doubts _____ it is true.

    A. whether   B. if   C. that   D. what

18. If you have high blood pressure, you should _____ eating too much salt.

    A. escape   B. suggest   C. relieve   D. avoid

19. _____ language, maths and history, the children are also taught music and art.

    A. Beside   B. Except   C. In spite   D. In addition to

20. I _____ the book in an old bookstore on Fourth Avenue.

    A. came on   B. came across   C. came up   D. came over

21. It is you _____ are responsible for the accident.

    A. who   B. which   C. whom   D. whoever

22. It was several minutes before I was _____ of what was happening.

    A. realized   B. aware   C. awake   D. curious

23. If you don't _____ yourself, you will be kept out of the classroom.

    A. believe   B. perform   C. behave   D. pretend

24. He came into the office with his hands _____ before him.

    A. crossed   B. crossing   C. being crossed   D. were crossed

25. I'm forever on a diet, _____ I put on weight easily.

    A. so   B. if   C. unless   D. since

Section B

Directions: *There are 10 incomplete statements here. You should fill in each blank with the proper form of the word given in brackets. Write the word or words in the corresponding space on the Answer Sheet.*

26. Without music, the world _____ (be) a dull place.

27. The books _____ (sell) fast in the bookstore now.

28. Can you tell me which you like _____ (good), coffee, milk or tea?

29. By our _____ (express), gestures and other body movements we send messages to those around us.

30. Titles are _____ (attach) to surnames in both Chinese and English.

31. Americans usually expect a thank-you at the end of your stay and polite _____ (consider) throughout your friendship.

32. Facts prove that the world's _____ (economy) development is not a win-lost game but one in which all can be winners.

33. Time _____ (permit), we'll come to see you again.

34. On _____ (introduce) to somebody, a British person often shakes hands with the stranger.

35. I had this hair done _____ (special) for your wedding.

Part III   Reading Comprehension

Directions: *This part is to test your reading ability. There are 5 tasks for you to fulfill. You should read the reading materials carefully and do the tasks as you are instructed.*

Task 1

Directions: *After reading the following passage, you will find 5 questions or unfinished statements, numbered 36 to 40. For each question or statement there are 4 choices marked A, B, C and D. You should make the correct choice and mark the corresponding letter on the Answer Sheet with a single line through the center.*

During McDonald's early years French fries were made from scratch every day. Fresh potatoes were peeled, cut into strings, and fried in the kitchens. As the chain expanded nationwide, in the mid-1960's, it sought to cut labor costs, reduce the number of supplies, and ensure that its fries tasted the same at every restaurant.

McDonald's began switching to frozen French fries in 1996, and few customers notice the difference. But the change had a profound effect on the nation's agriculture and diet. A familiar food had been transformed into a highly processed industrial commodity. McDonald's fries now come from huge manufacturing plants that can process two million pounds of potatoes every day. The expansion of McDonald's and the popularity of its mass-produced, low-cost fries changed the way that Americans eat.

The taste of McDonald's French fries played a crucial role in the chain's success—fries are much more profitable than hamburgers, and was long praised by customers, competitors, and even food critics. Their special taste does not come from the kind of potatoes McDonald's buys or the technology that processes them. The taste is determined by the cooking oil. The mixture of 7% cottonseed oil and 93% beef fat gave the fries their unique flavor.

36. What did McDonald's begin to do in 1996?

　　A. Expand chain.

　　B. Switch to frozen French fries.

　　C. Cut labor costs.

　　D. Reduce the number of supplies.

37. Which is the probable definition of the word "crucial" in Paragraph 3 Line 1?

　　A. Extremely important.

　　B. Cruel.

　　C. Excellent.

D. Perfect.
38. Where does the special taste of McDonald's French fries come from?
    A. Mixed cooking oil.
    B. Potatoes McDonald's buys.
    C. Technology that processes them.
    D. Beef fat.
39. With the expanding of the chain nationwide, which measures did McDonald's take in the mid-1960's?
    A. Seek to cut labor costs.
    B. Reduce the number of supplies.
    C. Ensure that its fries tasted the same.
    D. All of the above.
40. What is the most important in the chain's success?
    A. The taste.
    B. The kind of potatoes.
    C. The technology.
    D. The price.

Task 2

Directions: *Read the passage and decide whether the statements that follow are true or false. Write T for true or F for false.*

How man first learned to invent words is unknown. In other words, the beginning of language is a mystery. All we really know is that man, unlike animals, invented certain sounds to express thoughts and feelings, actions and things, so that they could communicate with each other; and that later they agreed on certain signs, which could be joined together to refer to those sounds, and which could be written down. Those sounds, spoken or written in letters, we call words. The power of words lies in the things they bring up before our minds. Words became filled with meaning for us by experience. The longer we live, the more certain words recall to the glad and sad things of our past; and the more we read and learn, the more the number of words that mean something to us increases.

(   ) 41. The beginning of language is a problem not yet settled.
(   ) 42. One of the reasons why man invented certain sounds to express thoughts and actions was that they could keep in touch with each other.
(   ) 43. The power of words lies in the things they bring up after our minds.
(   ) 44. Words are used to express feelings only.
(   ) 45. Words cannot be written down.

Task 3

Directions: *Read the passage and complete the outline that follows.*

In North America, when people greet each other, they generally say, "Hi, how are you?" This is NOT a question but rather a greeting. The expected answer is usually short, for example, "Fine," "OK," "Pretty good," "Not bad." A long, detailed answer or a negative answer would be strange unless you knew the person very well and could tell that the person expected more extensive information. People learning English may think that native speakers are impolite because they do not stop to have a conversation. But "How are you?" should be considered in the same way as "Hello." It's simply a greeting.

When people greet each other they say (46) _____.
People learning English may think it (47) _____ not to stop to have a conversation.
(48) _____ is usually preferred in greeting.
(49) _____ can be used in the same way as "Hello" in greeting.
We use long, detailed answer only when (50) _____.

Task 4

Directions: *Read the following list of terms for newspaper and find out the Chinese equivalents in the table after it.*

A. Entertainment   B. Letters to the Editor
C. The Arts   D. Local News
E. Business News   F. Movies
G. Community Calendar   H. Obituaries
I. Editorials   J. Police Report
K. Food   L. Real Estate
M. Health News   N. Sports
O. Recruitment advertisement

Example: (O) 招聘广告   (C) 艺术
51. (   ) 本地新闻   (   ) 娱乐
52. (   ) 电影   (   ) 读者来信
53. (   ) 社论   (   ) 商业新闻
54. (   ) 房地产   (   ) 美食
55. (   ) 体育   (   ) 讣告

Task 5

Directions: *The following is a passage. After reading it, you should give brief answers to the 5 questions (No. 56 to No. 60) that follow. The answers (in no more than 3 words) should be written after the corresponding numbers on the Answer Sheet.*

There are post offices in every city and nearly every village in the country. If you want to post an ordinary letter or a postcard, you needn't go to the post office, you can drop it into the nearest pillar box. You can recognize these pillar boxes easily for they're painted in special color. In some countries, they're painted green, but in England, they are painted red. Pillar boxes are emptied several times a day. If you want your letter to arrive more quickly, you can send it by airmail. Letters are delivered to your home or office by a postman.

If you want to buy some stamps, envelopes or postcards, or you want to send a parcel, you have to go to the post office. Before you send the parcel, you must hand it to the assistant, who will weigh it on scales and give you the necessary stamps. The amount you have to pay depends on the weight of the parcel.

In most post offices and in many streets, there are public telephone boxes. You can first lift the receiver, then put the coins due for the call into the slot, and finally dial the number.

56. How can you send an ordinary letter?
_____.

57. What's the color of pillar box in England?
_____.

58. How are letters delivered to you?
_____.

59. How do you send a parcel?
_____.

60. How do you make a call in a public telephone box?
_____.

Part Ⅳ Translation

Directions: *This part, numbered 61 through 65, is to test your ability to translate English into Chinese. After each of the sentences numbered 61 to 64, you will read four choices of suggested translation. You should choose the best translation and mark the corresponding letter on your Answer Sheet. And for the paragraph numbered 65, write your translation in the corresponding space on the Translation/ Composition Sheet.*

61. No one can use cell phones in any areas at the hospital where equipment might be influenced by the interference from cell phones.
    A. 在医院的任何区域都不得使用手机，因为会受到设备的干扰。
    B. 在医院的任何区域，手机会影响设备的使用，任何人都不得使用。
    C. 医院里没有人使用手机，因此不会影响设备的使用。
    D. 医院里，在干扰设备使用的任何区域，不得使用手机。

62. The Olympic Games are growing so big that most cities may not be able to host them in future.
    A. 奥运会规模越来越大，是为了大多数的城市将没有能力举办。
    B. 奥运会规模如此之大以致大多数城市将没有能力举办。
    C. 奥运会规模越来越大，大多数城市将无法举办。
    D. 奥运会发展越来越快结果大多数城市将没有能力举办。

63. It gives us much pleasure to send you the goods asked for in your letter of April 15th.
    A. 很高兴发去贵方4月15日来函索购的货物。
    B. 我们很高兴寄去你们4月15日来信询问的商品。
    C. 对寄去贵方4月15日来信索要的商品表示高兴。
    D. 我们十分高兴贵方4月15日来函询问我们的商品。

64. Many analysts suggest that this added pressure disproportionately touches the women, who already carry major responsibility for their own children.
    A. 对于那些已经承担了主要的抚养孩子的责任的妇女们，分析家认为这是雪上加霜。
    B. 许多分析家认为对于那些对孩子已经承担了主要责任的妇女来说，这加重了她们的压力。
    C. 许多分析家认为，对于那些已经承担了繁重的养儿育女责任的妇女们来说，这无疑是雪上加霜。
    D. 许多分析家建议加重承担养儿育女责任的妇女们的压力。

65. When people part, they usually say Good-bye, Bye-bye. Similar expressions are found in almost all languages. But in the more or less fixed conversational formulas that precede Good-bye, there may be interesting differences, as in Chinese when a distinguished guest drops in for a visit, or if the visitor is one with whom the hosts are not very familiar. The Chinese custom when such a guest leaves is for the hosts to see the visitor to the door or gateway. A smile and a gesture of farewell would be enough.

Part V Writing

Directions: *This part is to test your ability to do practical writing. You are required to write a letter of invitation with the information given below.*

1）你希望邀请 Mr. Right 参加晚会
2）告诉对方举办晚会的原因
3）告诉对方会安排哪些具体的活动

Unit 4

Part I Listening Comprehension

Section A

1-5: ACCAB

听力原稿

1. W: Good evening. What can I do for you, sir?

   M: I reserved a British suite three weeks ago. I'm Henry Bellow.

   Question: Where does the dialogue most probably take place?

2. M: The train is leaving in 10 minutes.

   W: It's ten thirty already. They are supposed to be here by now. I told everybody to meet here by 10:15.

   Question: When is the train leaving?

3. M: Prof. Smith asked me to go to his office after class.

   W: Then it seems we'll have to meet an hour later at the library.

   Question: What will the man do first after class?

4. M: Jane was late for her class this morning.

   W: It's nothing new for her.

   Question: What does the woman mean?

5. M: Hi, how about your college life in this semester?

   W: Very good. Now I'm a member of the English club.

   Question: What are they talking about?

Section B

6-10: ABDCD

听力原稿

Conversation 1

W: (picking up telephone) Rex Cinema. Can I help you?

M: Can you tell me what's on tonight, please?

W: We're showing The Sound of Music.

M: What time does it begin?

W: At eight o'clock.

M: How long does it last?

W: It lasts about two and a half hours.

M: How much are the tickets?

W: The seats upstairs cost four pounds and there are less expensive seats downstairs.

M: What's the film about?

W: It's about a singing family in Austria.

M: It sounds lovely, and I surely want to see it. Thank you very much. Goodbye.

W: Bye.

Question 6: What's the relationship between the two speakers?

Question 7: How much are the tickets downstairs?

Question 8: What is the man going to do next?

Conversation 2

W: Mr. Wang, I have seen your table lamps at the Trade Fair. I wish to order some for the US market. Could you please tell me more about it?

M: I'd be glad to. As a matter of fact, we have been thinking of selling our lamps to the United States as well. Well, we produce 200,000 table lamps a year. About half of them are sold to Asian countries.

W: What's your price?

M: 12 US dollars each.

W: Sounds reasonable. And is this the only model you produce?

M: No. We have several others. If you are interested, I'd like to take you around our factory.

W: That would be fine.

Question 9: Where has the woman seen the table lamps?

Question 10: How many table lamps are sold to Asian countries a year?

Section C

11. the Pacific Ocean

12. economic, scientific and technological

13. rail, highway

14. 400 million tons

15. the modern shipping need

听力原稿

The Port of Shanghai

Located in the middle of China's coastline and at the Changjiang River's outlet to the East China Sea, the Port of Shanghai faces the Pacific Ocean at the front and is supported by the city of Shanghai—the country's largest economic, scientific and technological center. Access to various parts of the country is provided by rail, highway and inland navigation, which enable the Port to transship the commodities from 20 Chinese provinces. Internationally, the Port has so far established trading and shipping relations with over 400 million ports in more than 160 countries and regions. Its annual cargo handling has reached 400 million tons, accounting for 35% of total via 15 China's major ports. Its international container handling capacity accounts for 33% of that of China's ports along the coast.

To accomplish the modern shipping need, the Port of Shanghai is quickening the construction and professional development of international container berths. The operation adopts advanced handling methods and computer technology, with container cranes at quayside and other heavy-duty machinery in the yard.

Question 11: Where does the Port of Shanghai face?
Question 12: What is the position of Shanghai in the country?
Question 13: By what is access to various parts of the country provided?
Question 14: How many does its annual cargo handling reach?
Question 15: Why is the Port of Shanghai quickening the construction and professional development of international container berths?

Part Ⅱ Vocabulary and Structure

Section A

16 – 20: CCDDB
21 – 25: ABCAD

Section B

26. would be   27. are selling   28. best   29. expressions   30. attached
31. considerations 32. economic   33. permitting 34. being introduced 35. specially

Part Ⅲ Reading Comprehension

36 – 40: BAADA
41 – 45: TTFFF

46. Hi, how are you?

47. impolite

48. A short answer

49. How are you?

50. we knew the person very well and could tell that the person expected more extensive information

51. D, A   52. F, B   53. I, E   54. L, K   55. N, H

56. Drop it into the nearest pillar box.

57. Red.

58. Delivered by postman.

59. Go to the post office, hand it to the assistant to have it weigh, and stick stamps on it.

60. Lift the receiver, put the money into the slot, and dial the number.

Part Ⅳ Translation

61-64：DBAC

65. 人们分手时通常说再见。几乎所有的语言中都有类似的说法。但在说再见之前，还有些客套语很有意思，各种语言也不尽相同。如有贵客或不大熟的人来访或串门儿，客人离开时，按中国的习惯，主人要把客人送到房门口或大门口。其实，微微一笑并作个表示再见的手势就可以了。

Part Ⅴ Writing

参考范文

Dear Mr. Right,

　　I am greatly honored to formally invite you to participate in Mr. Guo Jing's wedding ceremony with Ms. Huang Rong to be held at Beijing Grand Hotel from 8 to 10 p.m. on April 1, 2007.

　　As you are a close friend of us, we would very much like you to attend the celebration and share our joy. The occasion will start at seven o'clock in the evening, with the showing of their wedding ceremony. This will be followed by a dinner party. At around ten, we will hold a small musical soiree, at which a band will perform some works by Bach and Strauss.

　　If you do not have any prior appointment on April 1, we look forward to the pleasure of your company.

Yours sincerely,

Li Ming

Unit 5

Part I Listening Comprehension

Section A

Directions: *In this section, you will hear 10 short conversations. At the end of each conversation, a question will be asked about what was said. Both the conversations and the questions will be spoken twice. After each question there will be a pause. During the pause you must read the four choices marked A, B, C and D, and decide which is the best answer. Then mark the corresponding letter on the Answer Sheet with a single line through the center.*

1. A. At 10:00.　　B. At 9:00.　　C. At 9:15.　　D. At 9:30.
2. A. A clerk.　　B. A teacher.　　C. A typist.　　D. A secretary.
3. A. Reporter and editor.　　　　　B. Student and teacher.
   C. Writer and publisher.　　　　　D. Secretary and boss.
4. $ 3.50.　　B. $ 3.15.　　C. $ 3.　　D. $ 2.50.
5. A. Ask the air hostess for a change.　　B. Move to another part of the place.
   C. Sit where there is fresh air.　　　　D. Put out his cigarette.
6. A. In a bus.　　B. In a shop.　　C. In a restaurant.　　D. In a hospital.
7. A. England.　　B. America.　　C. Australia.　　D. France.
8. A. That tomatoes don't taste good.
   B. That he should try tomatoes because they really are good.
   C. That tomatoes are good for his health.
   D. That she likes tomatoes but he probably wouldn't like them.
9. A. The red one.　　　　　　B. The green one.
   C. The cheaper one.　　　　D. The one on the right.
10. A. To sell her car.　　　　　　B. To have her car washed.
    C. To have her car re-fueled.　　D. To have her car checked.

Section B:

Directions: *In this section, you will hear a short passage. At the end of the passage, you will hear two questions. Both the passage and the questions will be spoken twice. After you hear one question, you must choose the best answer from the four choices marked A, B, C and D. Then mark the corresponding letter on the Answer Sheet with a single line through the center.*

Questions 11 to 12 are based on the following passage you have just heard.

11. A. Father and mother.   B. Boyfriend and girlfriend.
    C. Husband and wife.   D. Brother and sister.

12. A. They have different shopping habits.
    B. They don't have enough time.
    C. They can never find bargains.
    D. They want to wait for a better deal.

Section C

Directions: *In this section, you will hear a passage three times. Listen carefully during the first reading. Then listen to the passage again. When it is being read the second time, you should fill in the six blanks numbered from S1) to S6) with the exact words or phrases you have just heard. Finally, when the passage is read for the third time, you should check what you have written.*

The younger members of most American families don't like foreign food. They like hamburgers. Most American children and (S1) _____ love to eat it any time of the day or night. Millions of hamburgers are eaten every year. Thousands of roadside restaurants prepare and sell them. These are not really restaurants (S2) _____; they often have little space for tables and chairs. Many people buy their hamburgers and take them (S3) _____ to eat, or eat them in their cars.

Sometimes it is not (S4) _____ to go inside in order to buy the hamburgers. They are ordered through a window in the restaurant and then are (S5) _____ out through the window to the waiting customer. Sometimes the customer doesn't even have to get out of his car.

When an American family travels (S6) _____, this is almost always the custom that the younger members of the family miss hamburgers most.

Part II Vocabulary and structure

Directions: *There are 20 incomplete sentences in this part. For each sentence there are four choices marked A, B, C and D. Choose the one answer that best completes the sentence. Then mark the corresponding letter on the Answer Sheet with a single line through the center.*

13. It is obvious that concrete bridges are superior ____ wooden bridges.

A. with　　　　B. to　　　　　　C. against　　　　D. for
14. During the past twenty years, there have been ____ changes in the country.
　　A. permanent　　B. powerful　　C. imaginary　　　D. dramatic
15. The young man who came to your rescue in the accident was ____ my friend.
　　A. no other than　B. not other than　C. none other than　D. less other than
16. Beijing is ____ that we can hardly visit all the beautiful places in two or three days.
　　A. such a large city　B. such large a city　C. so a large city　D. a such large city
17. The Italian boy was regarded as a hero ____ he gave his life for his country.
　　A. according to　B. because of　C. on account of　D. because
18. Not until I began to work ____ how much time I had wasted.
　　A. didn't I realize　B. did I realize　C. I didn't realize　D. I realize
19. ____ of the students in Class One ____ already seen the movie.
　　A. Three fourths, have　　　　　B. Third fourths, have
　　C. Four thirds, have　　　　　　D. Three fourths, has
20. Was it because there was too much noise ____ he wanted to move to the suburbs?
　　A. where　　　B. then　　　　C. that　　　　　D. why
21. No matter ____ happened, he would not say a word.
　　A. whatever　　B. what　　　　C. when　　　　　D. where
22. Those who let children who are ____ go swimming in the river are foolish.
　　A. too young to　B. so young　　C. not old enough to　D. young enough
23. We have come to the conclusion ____ this summer will be much hotter than before.
　　A. for　　　　B. but　　　　　C. that　　　　　D. when
24. Dick picked up the broken cup and tried ____ to put them together.
　　A. in person　　B. in vain　　　C. in time　　　　D. in order
25. The number of the trucks produced in our factory this year ____ in yours.
　　A. is more than that　　　　　　B. are more that those
　　C. is larger than that　　　　　　D. are larger than those
26. Another driver had just driven into the back of Bob's car ____ he was waiting at some traffic lights.
　　A. since　　　　B. once　　　　C. while　　　　　D. as
27. A beautiful ____ of the whole town from the top floor of Great Hotel made a deep impression on me.
　　A. view　　　　B. vision　　　　C. look　　　　　D. appearance
28. Because of ____ you have done, things became much worse.
　　A. that　　　　B. what　　　　C. which　　　　　D. whom

29. All the letters ____, Bethe took them to the post office.

    A. had been writing B. having been written C. wrote D. had written

30. The little boy dare not tell his parents what he did, ____ they would not forgive him.

    A. in case   B. for fear that   C. that   D. since

31. We've tested three hundred types of boot, ____ is completely waterproof.

    A. no of which   B. none of which   C. some of that   D. neither of them

32. We must stop now. It is time we ____ home.

    A. have gone   B. are going   C. were going   D. will go

Part III Reading Comprehension

Directions: *There are four passages in this part. Each passage is followed by five questions or unfinished statements. For each question, there are four choices marked A, B, C and D. You should choose the best answer. Then mark the corresponding letter on the Answer Sheet with a single line through the center.*

Passage 1

Strange things happen to time when you travel, because the earth is divided into twenty-four time zones, one hour apart. You can have days with more or fewer than twenty-four hours, and weeks with more or fewer than seven days.

If you make a five-day trip across the Atlantic Ocean, your ship enters a different time zone every day. As you enter each zone, the time changes every hour. Traveling west, you set your clock back; traveling east, you set it ahead. Each day of your trip has either twenty-five or twenty-three hours.

If you travel by ship across the Pacific, you cross the International Date Line. By agreement, this is the point where a new day begins. When you cross the line, you change your calendar one full day, backward or forward. Traveling east, today becomes yesterday and traveling west, it is tomorrow!

33. When you travel, you will find something strange about time. You may find ____.

    A. there are only 23 hours in a day   B. there are 8 days in a week

    C. there are one more hour in a day   D. all of the above

34. The difference in time between neighboring time zones is ____.

    A. seven days   B. 24 hours

    C. one hour   D. more than seven days

35. If you cross the ocean, going east, you set your watch ____.

    A. ahead one hour in each new time zone

    B. ahead one hour for the whole trip

C. back one full day for the whole trip

D. back by 24 hours

36. The International Date Line is the name for ____.

   A. the beginning of any new time zone

   B. any point where time changes by one hour

   C. the point where a new day begins

   D. any time zone in the Pacific Ocean

37. The best title for this passage is ____.

   A. Trip Across the Atlantic

   B. How Time Changes Around the World

   C. Crossing the International Date Line

   D. How Time Zones Were Set Up

Passage 2

Mrs. Peters stopped playing the piano when she began to work. She had lived in a very small flat, and there had been no room for a piano. But when she married, she had a new flat which was big enough for one. So she decided to get one and her husband agreed and helped her. She saved some money, and her parents gave her a generous amount of money for her birthday. Then she went to a shop and said, "I'll choose whichever piano does not cost too much and fits into my living room."

When she had paid for the piano, the shop assistant asked her if she would like him to get it tuned （调音） every few months. Mrs. Peters agreed.

A few months later she heard from the shop that a man was coming to tune the piano at ten that morning. Now she had not cleaned the house yet, so it was dusty and untidy. Mrs. Peters hated having even the least amount of dirt, and felt ashamed whenever strange people saw her house like that. So she had to hurry to clean everything carefully. It meant a lot of effort, and it made her hot and tired, but anyhow, by the time the man arrived, everything was finished.

She opened the door, and the man was standing there with a big dog. "Good morning," the man said politely, "will it disturb （打扰） you if I bring my dog in, please? I'm blind, and he leads me wherever I go."

38. Mrs. Peters stopped playing the piano ____.

   A. because she began to work

   B. when she had no room to live in

   C. because her flat was too small for a piano

   D. when she got married

39. Mrs. Peters was soon able to buy a piano because ____.

   A. her parents gave her all the money for it

B. she saved enough money for it

C. her husband gave her the money

D. she saved some money and her relatives gave her the rest

40. One morning, ____.

    A. the man was coming to tune her piano

    B. Mrs. Peters received a telephone call from the shop

    C. the piano was sent to her house at 10

    D. Mrs. Peters was going to clean the house

41. "It meant a lot of effort, and it made her hot and tired." Here "it" refers to ____.

    A. hating dirt

    B. cleaning everything

    C. waiting for the man

    D. feeling ashamed of the dirty and untidy house

42. Mrs. Peters had wasted her time getting everything clean as ____.

    A. the dog would dirty the house

    B. the piano tuner could see nothing in the house

    C. the dog disturbed Mrs. Peters

    D. the piano tuner always took the dog

Passage 3

The dog has always been considered man's best friend. Always noted for being particular faithful in watching over children, he also has his place by the fireside, in the cow pasture, on the sheep range, and beside the hunter or blind. He is easy to train, works hard, and often performs astonishing feats. And in the frozen polar regions, he was once the principal motive power, before being largely replaced by the plane and helicopter.

Because he howls or whines in the presence of impending death, the dog was once thought to have supernatural powers and believed to be capable of seeing gods and ghosts invisible to people. Actually, the basis for these beliefs lies in the dog's sensitivity to people's feelings and his superior hearing ability and sense of smell, which enable him to detect signs hidden from human observation. His record of saving lives is outstanding, for he often gives warning of fire and other dangers not noticed by his master.

The dog's major contribution, however, has been to medical research. Both his diet and his structure are comparable to those of the human being, and so he has been the subject, of countless demonstrations and experiments. Open-heart surgery has been made possible largely because of the dog. But his sacrifice has repaid his own species as well by safeguarding it from rabies（狂犬病）, distemper, and other diseases.

43. The dog has always been noted for ____.
    A. protecting children   B. assisting shepherds
    C. helping hunters   D. herding a cattle
44. The dog is useful to herders because he is ____.
    A. loyal   B. easily trained
    C. hard working   D. all of the above
45. The dog probably whines in the presence of death because he can ____.
    A. see ghosts and spirits   B. give warning of danger
    C. sense unhappiness around him   D. perform astonishing feats
46. The dog has been of most valuable to people in the development of ____.
    A. a treatment of rabies   B. open-heart surgery
    C. a cure for distemper   D. all of the above
47. The article does not say whether the scientists' experiments with dog have ____.
    A. benefited animals other than dogs
    B. served people
    C. helped other dogs
    D. contributed to medical knowledge

Passage 4

Almost every family buys at least one copy of a newspaper every day. Some people subscribe to as many as two or three different newspapers. But why do people read newspapers?

Five hundred years ago, news of important happenings—battles lost and won, kings or rulers overthrown or killed—took months and even years to travel from one country to another. The news passed by word of mouth and was never accurate. Today we can read in our newspapers of important events that occur in faraway countries on the same day they happen.

Apart from supplying news from all over the world, newspapers give us a lot of other useful information. There are weather reports, radio, television and film guides, book reviews, stories, and, of course, advertisements. There are all sorts of advertisements. The bigger ones are put in by large companies to bring attention to their products. They pay the newspapers thousands of dollars for their advertising space, but it is worth the money, for news of their products goes into almost every home in the country. For those who produce newspapers, advertisements are also important. Money earned from advertisements makes it possible for them to sell their newspapers at a low price and still make a profit.

48. The habit of reading newspapers is ____.
    A. widespread   B. found among a few families
    C. not popular   D. uncommon

49. In the past, news was ____.
    A. sent by telegraph   B. sent by letter
    C. passed from one person to another   D. sent by telephone
50. The money spent on advertisements is ____.
    A. wasted   B. not much
    C. worthwhile   D. of no use to anyone
51. Which of the following statements is not true?
    A. Five hundred years ago news did not take a long time to reach other countries.
    B. Large companies put big advertisements in the newspapers to make their products known.
    C. The news that we need in our newspapers is up-to-date.
    D. Though the newspapers are sold at a low price, their owners still gain profit.
52. The phrase "subscribe to" in the second sentence means ____.
    A. contribute to   B. write lo
    C. pay for receiving   D. appreciate

Part IV Translation

Directions: *This part, numbered 61 through 65, is to test your ability to translate English into Chinese. After each of the sentences numbered 61 to 64, you will read four choices of suggested translation. You should choose the best translation and mark the corresponding letter on your Answer Sheet. And for the paragraph numbered 65, write your translation in the corresponding space on the Translation/ Composition Sheet.*

1. Strange things happen to time when you travel, because the earth is divided into twenty-four time zones, one hour apart.
2. When she had paid for the piano, the shop assistant asked her if she would like him to get it tuned (调音) every few months.
3. And in the frozen polar regions, he was once the principal motive power, before being largely replaced by the plane and helicopter.
4. They pay the newspapers thousands of dollars for their advertising space, but it is worth the money, for news of their products goes into almost every home in the country.

Part V Writing

Directions: *For this part, you are allowed thirty minutes to write a passage under the title* **The Value of Time**. *You should write at least 120 words in three paragraphs and base your writing on the outline below in Chinese.*

1. 有人说"时间就是金钱"。
2. 我们应充分利用时间。
3. 我的看法。

Words for reference: precious, limited, devote, acquire

Unit 5

Part I   Listening Comprehension

Section A

1–5: CCBAB

6–10: CABBD

听力原稿

1. M: Hello. This is Tom Davis. I have an appointment with Mrs. Jones for nine o'clock this morning, but I'm afraid I'll have to be about fifteen minutes late.

   W: That's alright, Mr. Davis. She doesn't have another appointment until ten o'clock.

   Q: When will Mr. Davis most probably meet with Mrs. Jones?

2. M: Hello, Jean. I hear that you have a job as a typist at the university.

   W: Yes, I work at the office every morning. I also do filing and sometimes write letters.

   Q: What kind of job does the woman have?

3. M: I think if I learn enough vocabulary, I won't have any trouble using English.

   W: That's not necessarily so. You'll see in my lecture today that language consists of much more than just vocabulary.

   Q: What's the probable relationship between the two speakers?

4. W: I thought that these typewriter ribbons cost three dollars.

   M: They used to, but the price has gone up fifty cents.

   Q: How much do the typewriter ribbons cost now?

5. M: I can hardly breathe. Would you please put your cigarette out?

   W: I'm sorry that I'm bothering you, but this is the smoking section. Why don't you ask the hostess to change your seat?

   Q: What does the woman think the man should do?

6. W: Well, now. Before we order, shall we agree that we each pay our own bill?

   M: All right.

   Q: Where are the two speakers?

7. W: Are you an American?

   M: No, my family moved to Australia from England 50 years ago. I'm an Australian.

   Q: Where did the family come from 50 years ago?

8. M: I've never tried tomatoes but I'm sure I wouldn't like them if I did.

   W: You don't know what you are missing.

   Q: What was the woman telling the man?

9. W: How about the red one on the right? It's cheaper.

   M: The green one on the left is much better, though it's more expensive.

   Q: Which one does the man want to buy?

10. M: Good morning, Mrs. Smith. What can we do for you?

    W: Could you please look over my car? I've just noticed that it's been using up a lot of gas lately.

    Q: What did the woman want to do?

Section B

11. C   12. A

听力原稿

My husband, Tom, is a born shopper. He loved to look at things and to touch them. He likes to compare prices between the same items in different stores. He would never think of buying anything without looking around in several stores. I, on the other hand, am not a shopper. I regards shopping as boring and unpleasant. If I like something and can afford it, I buy it instantly. I never take a time to look around for a good sale or a better deal.

Bargains don't interest me. Needless to say, Tom and I never go shopping together. The experience would be too painful for both of us. When it comes to shopping, we go our separate ways.

11. What's the relationship between Tom and the speaker?
12. Why doesn't Tom ever go shopping with the speaker?

Section C

S1: teenagers   S2: in the usual sense   S3: home
S4: necessary   S5: handed   S6: abroad

听力原稿

The younger members of most American families don't like foreign food. They like hamburgers. Most American children and teenagers love to eat it any time of the day or night. Millions of hamburgers are eaten every year. Thousands of roadside restaurants prepare and sell them. These are not really restaurants in the usual sense; they often have little space for tables and chairs. Many people buy their hamburgers and take them home to eat, or eat them in their cars.

Sometimes it is not necessary to go inside in order to buy the hamburgers. They are ordered through a window in the restaurant and then are handed out through the window to the waiting customer. Sometimes the customer doesn't even have to get out of his car.

When an American family travels abroad, this is almost always the custom that the younger members of the family miss hamburgers most.

Part Ⅱ   Vocabulary and Structure

13. B   14. D   15. A   16. A   17. D   18. B   19. A   20. C   21. B   22. B
23. C   24. B   25. C   26. C   27. A   28. B   29. B   30. B   31. B   32. C

Part Ⅲ   Reading Comprehension

33. D   34. C   35. A   36. C   37. B   38. C   39. D   40. B   41. B   42. B
43. A   44. D   45. C   46. B   47. A   48. A   49. C   50. C   51. A   52. C

Part Ⅳ   Translation

1. 你旅行时，时间会发生奇妙的事情，因为地球分为24个时区，一小时为一个时区。
2. 当她付了钢琴的钱以后，那位店员问她是否希望他每隔几个月给她的钢琴调音。
3. 在常年结冰的北极和南极地区，他（狗）在主要被飞机和直升机代替之前曾经是主要的运输动力。
4. 他们要为他们的广告所占的版面付给报纸数千美元的费用。但是这是值得的，因为他们的产品几乎进入了那个国家的每一个家庭。

Part Ⅴ   Writing

The value of Time

As a popular saying goes, "Time is money." In fact, time is more precious than money. When money is spent, you can earn it back if you want to. However, when time is gone, it will never come back.

As the pace of modern life continues to accelerate, our time seems quite limited. But there are a lot of things to be done in our lives. We should make full use of our time to fulfill what is useful to us. As students we should devote most of our time to our studies. In this way can we acquire new knowledge and skills necessary for our future career.

In my opinion, wasting time means wasting our valuable life. But many of us don't realize this. They think time is inexhaustible. But I'm not in favor of such a view. I think we should never put off what can be done today until tomorrow.

Unit 6

Part I Listening Comprehension

Directions: *This part is to test your listening ability. It consists of 3 sections.*

Section A

Directions: *This section is to test your ability to understand short dialogues. There are 5 recorded dialogues in it. After each dialogue, there is a recorded question. Both the dialogues and questions will be spoken only once. When you hear a question, you should decide on the correct answer from the 4 choices marked A, B, C and D given in your test paper. Then you should mark the corresponding letter on the Answer Sheet with a single line through the center.*

1. A. Don't mention it.   B. At about 2 o'clock.
   C. Thanks for your help.   D. It's 54576862.
2. A. I agree.   B. Tea, please.
   C. My pleasure.   D. No problem.
3. A. Go on, please.   B. Take care.
   C. I'd love to.   D. You are welcome.
4. A. It's interesting.   B. Here it is.
   C. I don't think so.   D. Yes, let's do it.
5. A. Sorry to hear that.   B. Yes, of course.
   C. See you later.   D. Nice to meet you.

Section B

Directions: *This section is to test your ability to understand short conversations. There are 5 recorded conversations in it. After each conversation, there is a recorded question. Both the conversations and questions will be spoken two times. When you hear a question, you should decide on the correct answer from the 4 choices marked A, B, C and D given in your test paper. Then you should mark the corresponding letter on the Answer Sheet with a single line through the center.*

6. A. When to catch the train.   B. Where to buy the ticket.
   C. How to reach the airport.   D. Which bus stop to get off.
7. A. She was ill at that time.   B. She was busy with her work.
   C. She forgot about the meeting. D. She was preparing for a trip.
8. A. Write a report.   B. Type a report.
   C. Send a report.   D. Read a report.
9. A. Pay his bill.   B. Show his business card.
   C. Fill in a form.   D. Make a phone call.
10. A. Project engineer.   B. Shop assistant.
    C. Computer programmer.   D. Marketing manager.

Section C

Directions: *In this section you will hear a recorded short passage. The passage is printed in the test paper, but with some words or phrases missing. The passage will be read three times. During the second reading, you are required to put the missing words or phrases on the Answer Sheet in order of the numbered blanks according to what you hear. The third reading is for you to check your writing. Now the passage will begin.*

When you are starting a small business, you should write a business plan. Writing a business plan is the most important ___(11)___. This is how people will think about your business. When you ___(12)___ support from a bank, the bank will read your plan seriously before it gives you any help. Even if you're starting the business with ___(13)___, you will still need to have a written plan to help ___(14)___ your business. The marketing plan is the important part of a business plan. It will help you to sell the products or ___(15)___.

Part II Vocabulary and Structure

Directions: *This part is to test your ability to construct grammatically correct sentences. It consists of 2 sections.*

Section A

Directions: *In this section, there are 10 incomplete sentences. You are required to complete each one by deciding on the most appropriate word or words from the 4 choices marked A, B, C and D. Then you should mark the corresponding letter on the Answer Sheet with a single line through the center.*

16. We will have to pay them a large ____ of money for their service.

A. size   B. set   C. amount   D. series
17. I'd appreciate it if you could tell me how ____ the machine.
   A. operate   B. to operate   C. operating   D. operated
18. I'm sorry to tell you that the materials you wanted are ____.
   A. taken off   B. put up   C. sold out   D. got off
19. It is obvious that these small businesses are ____ need of technical support.
   A. in   B. on   C. with   D. to
20. ____ I am concerned, it is important to get a job first.
   A. As long as   B. As well as   C. As soon as   D. As far as
21. Some companies might not let you rent a car ____ you have a credit card.
   A. where   B. because   C. since   D. unless
22. In his opinion, success in life mainly ____ on how we get along with other people.
   A. keeps   B. depends   C. insists   D. spends
23. We ____ building the bridge by the end of next month.
   A. are finishing   B. have finished   C. would finish   D. will have finished
24. Our company's service is ____ in nearly 80 countries around the world.
   A. available   B. natural   C. relative   D. careful
25. It was in Jonson's hotel ____ the business meeting was held last year.
A. this   B. that   C. what   D. which

Section B

Directions: *There are also 10 incomplete statements here. You should fill in each blank with the proper form of the word given in brackets.*

26. To start your own business is usually (cheap) ____ than to buy one.
27. The foreign professor spoke slowly and (clear) ____ so that we could follow him.
28. The money (borrow) ____ from the bank has already been paid back.
29. The (manage) ____ said that their company wouldn't be responsible for the loss of the goods.
30. When we get his telephone number, we (tell) ____ you immediately.
31. It won't make any (different) ____ whether he comes to the meeting or not.
32. The machine should (test) ____ before it is put to use.
33. We look forward to (meet) ____ you and wish you every success in your career.
34. My (person) ____ experience suggests that we should contact the customers first.
35. After the lecture yesterday, they (realize) ____ how important company culture was.

Part III Reading Comprehension

Directions: *This part is to test your reading ability. There are 5 tasks for you to fulfill. You should read the reading materials carefully and do the tasks as you are instructed.*

Task 1

Directions: *After reading the following passage, you will find 5 questions or unfinished statements, numbered 36 to 40. For each question or statement there are 4 choices marked A, B, C and D.*

A car is made up of more than 30,000 parts. Each part in a new car is as weak as a baby. So a new car requires proper care and servicing. If you're unfamiliar with the parts, you have to read through the owner's instructions carefully.

First of all, the brakes (刹车) of your car are important for safety (安全) reasons. Having them checked regularly can reduce the risks of accidents. Another important thing to consider is engine care. Always remember that the life and performance of your car engine depend on the engine oil. Replace the engine oil when recommended. If you feel the engine is very hot especially during summer it is probably because the cooling system doesn't work well. You'd better get the cooling system serviced before the start of summer.

In a word, timely and proper servicing is an important task for car owners. Good servicing can not only extend the life of your newborn baby, but also ensure your safety, and the safety of those who share the road with you.

36. To get familiar with the parts of a new car, the owner should _____.

    A. regard the car as a new-born baby

    B. have the car serviced before driving it

    C. read through the instructions carefully

    D. examine all of the parts of the new car

37. The brakes should be checked regularly _____.

    A. to avoid accidents   B. to raise speed

    C. to reduce cost   D. to save gas

38. For a car engine to work long and well, the owner should _____.

    A. replace the engine oil as recommended

    B. reduce the use of the car in summer

    C. clean the engine parts regularly

    D. change the brakes frequently

39. It is recommended to have the cooling system checked when _____.

    A. you buy a new car   B. summer is coming

    C. the engine oil is replaced   D. the brakes are out of order

40. The last paragraph tells us that the purpose of carefully servicing a car is _____.

   A. to let you sell your car at a good price

   B. to extend its life and ensure safety

   C. to reduce the cost of car servicing

   D. to make the car run faster

Task 2

Directions: *This task is the same as Task 1. The 5 questions or unfinished statements are numbered 41 to 45.*

Ticket-booking Policies

General Policies

Once the flight ticket has been issued, the name on the ticket cannot be changed.

Ticket is non-refundable (不能退款的).

Please review your itinerary (行程安排) immediately. If any problems arise before or during your trip, you must call our booking offices right away. If you wait until you return, it's too late.

There are times when we are unable to confirm a booking. In that case we will attempt to reach you by phone and e-mail. You must call us back within 48 hours or we may not be able to offer you the booking price.

Change Policies

If you change your booking, airlines may charge a fee— $150 to $200.

Some tickets do not allow any changes.

Need to change or cancel your trip? Visit our website to check the fees and rules before you decide.

Cancellation (取消) Policies

If you cancel your booking you will not receive any money back.

You may apply part of your ticket price towards future travel (for a limited time, usually a year).

41. According to the policies, the name on the ticket cannot be changed once the ticket is ____.

   A. booked   B. issued   C. cancelled   D. confirmed

42. If you have any problems during a trip, you should ____.

   A. ask for a refund   B. change your itinerary

   C. call the booking office   D. return the ticket to the office

43. What happens when your ticket booking cannot be confirmed?

   A. You should make another booking immediately.

   B. You can change your booking free of charge.

   C. You will be informed by phone and e-mail.

D. You will still enjoy the booking price.

44. If you want to change a booking, you may have to pay _____.

   A. 10% of the booking price   B. a fee of $150 to $200
   C. half the ticket price   D. a fixed fee

45. Which of the following statements is TRUE according to the cancellation policies?

   A. You can use part of the ticket price for future travel.
   B. You can refund the money from the booking office.
   C. You can keep the booking effective for one year.
   D. You cannot cancel your booking in any case.

Task 3

Directions: *Read the following passage. After reading it, you should complete the information by filling in the blanks marked 46 to 50 in no more than 3 words in the table below.*

If you are staying in the UK for more than 6 months, it may be useful to open a UK bank account. There are a lot of advantages of having a UK current (checking) account:

Paying bills

Many landlords prefer to collect rent directly from a bank account.

You may be able to obtain cheaper services if you pay bills directly from a bank account, e.g. telephone/gas/water/electricity.

If you are given a chequebook, you can also write cheques as a safe way of paying for things.

Cash

You can easily obtain money from cash machines, or pay directly from your account using a debit card（借记卡）.

Saving money

It is generally cheaper to use a UK account than it is to pay by credit card（信用卡）or withdraw（提取）cash from a foreign bank.

Employment

If you work in the UK, some employers require you to have a bank account so that you can get your pay.

Advantages of UK Current Account

Paying bills: 1) to pay rent directly from _____(46)_____

2) to obtain _____(47)_____ services

3) to pay for things with cheques safely

Cash: 1) to obtain money from _____(48)_____ easily

2) to pay directly from your account

Saving money: cheaper to use a ___(49)___ account

Employment: to get your ___(50)___ through a bank account

Task 4

Directions: *The following is a list of terms related to the human resources management. After reading it, you are required to find the items equivalent to（与……等同）those given in Chinese in the table below.*

A—Employee relations
C—Night shift
E—Human resources management
G—Employment injury insurance
I—Annual salary
K—Contract of service
M—Sick leave
O—Unemployment insurance
Q—Quality management

B—Basic salary
D—Attendance book
F—Work permit
H—Housing fund
J—Year-end bonus
L—Evaluation of employees
N—Coffee break
P—Minimum wage

Examples: (L) 员工考核   (E) 人力资源管理

51. (　　) 年薪   (　　) 最低工资
52. (　　) 服务合同   (　　) 员工关系
53. (　　) 工伤保险   (　　) 失业保险
54. (　　) 病假   (　　) 工作许可证
55. (　　) 住房基金   (　　) 基本工资

Task 5

Directions: *The following is a letter of recommendation. After reading it, you are required to complete the answers that follow the questions (No. 56 to No. 60).*

Dear Mr. Brown,

  Thank you for your letter of 6 September regarding Mr. John Green who has been employed by this company for the past 10 years.

  Mr. Green served his apprenticeship （学徒） with Vickers Tools Ltd. in Manchester, followed by a three-year course of engineering for Production Engineers. He is technically well-qualified and for the past five years has been our Assistant Works Manager responsible for production and related business in our Sheffield factory. In all his job duties he has shown himself to be hard-working, responsible and in every way a very dependable employee.

  I can strongly recommend Mr. Green as I feel sure that if he were to be chosen to manage your factory in Nairobi he would bring to his work a true atmosphere of teamwork, which would be found necessary and helpful by all who would work with him.

Sincerely yours,
Tom Smith

56. How long has Mr. Green been employed by the writer's company?

For _____.

57. What kind of course did Mr. Green take?

A three-year course in engineering for _____.

58. What job position has Mr. Green held in the past five years? _____.

59. What does the writer think of Mr. Green as an employee?

He is hard-working, _____ and dependable.

60. What is the purpose of this letter?

To _____ Mr. Green to manage a factory in Nairobi.

Part IV Translation

Directions: *This part, numbered 61 through 65, is to test your ability to translate English into Chinese. After each of the sentences numbered 61 to 64, you will read four choices of suggested translation. You should choose the best translation and mark the corresponding letter on your Answer Sheet. And for the paragraph numbered 65, write your translation in the corresponding space on the Translation/ Composition Sheet.*

61. With fuel prices going up, car buyers are changing their idea of buying a car.

   A. 燃料的价格正在随着购车者买车想法的改变而上涨。

   B. 燃料价格的涨落正在不断改变着购车族人群的构成。

   C. 随着燃料价格的上涨，购车者买车的想法正在改变。

   D. 燃料价格上涨的时候，购车者买车的想法也会改变。

62. You have to raise the quality of your products because buyers in those countries are very much quality-minded.

   A. 你们的当务之急是提高产品质量，因为这些买家对质量都很挑剔。

   B. 质量第一对你们很重要，因为所有国家的人都非常在乎产品质量。

   C. 你们要让那些国家的买家对产品感兴趣，就必须要明确质量优先。

   D. 你们必须提高产品质量，因为那些国家买家的质量意识都非常强。

63. Trading companies need to ensure their ability to handle orders efficiently, making an online system an essential sales channel.

   A. 贸易公司需要得到公司的明确指示，才能把重要的网络销售系统建立起来。

B. 贸易公司需要保证他们有能力来处理订单，才能使网上销售渠道变得重要。

C. 贸易公司需确保拥有高效处理订单的能力，使在线系统成为重要销售渠道。

D. 贸易公司需要有办法来执行公司的指令，以便建立起基本的网络销售系统。

64. It is necessary to have a good understanding of all the terms and conditions before signing a contract.

A. 先好好讨论一下各项条款，看是否有必要签合同。

B. 在签订合同之前必须充分理解合同中的所有条款。

C. 对所有合同条款都已正确理解，现在可以签合同。

D. 合同的所有条款要更好地解释之后方能签字生效。

65. Thank you for coming to the job interview at our office yesterday.

Within two weeks we will tell you our decision on your application. We want you to know that we will seriously consider your application. If, for some reason, we cannot offer you a position at this time, we will keep your application on record. When there is a job opening, we will inform you immediately.

Part V　Writing

Directions：*This part is to test your ability to do practical writing. You are required to complete a Telephone Message according to the following instructions given in Chinese.*

66. 说明：假定你是秘书 Linda Wang，请按下列内容填写给经理 John Brown 的电话留言。

内容：

1. 来电人：APP 公司 Mr. Peter Margin

2. 来电时间：12 月 13 日上午 10：30

3. 来电内容：Mr. Peter Margin 将于下周一去纽约，下周没有时间与您见面。他希望在本周五上午 9：30 能见到您，讨论双方合作事宜。您是否有空？希望您收到留言后尽早回电给 Mr. Peter Margin。

Unit 6

Part I Listening Comprehension

Section A

1-5: DBCAB

听力原稿

1. Q: Can I have your phone number, please?
2. Q: Which would you prefer, tea or coffee?
3. Q: Would you like to come for dinner tonight?
4. Q: How do you like the work here?
5. Q: Excuse me, do I have to pay in cash?

Section B

6-10: CAACD

听力原稿

6. W: May I help you, sir?

    M: Yes. Could you tell me how to get to the airport?

    Q: What does the man want to know?

7. M: Did you attend the meeting last Friday?

    W: No, I didn't, because I was ill.

    Q: Why didn't the woman attend the meeting?

8. W: Do you want me to write the report for you?

    M: No, thanks. I'll do it myself.

    Q: What will the man do?

9. M: I'd like a room for three nights, please?

    W: OK. Please fill in this form.

    Q: What is the man going to do?

10. W: What company are you from, Mr. Wang?
    M: ACC Company. I'm the marketing manager.
    Q: What is Mr. Wang's job?

Section C

11. step   12. are looking for   13. your own money   14. develop   15. your services

听力原稿

When you are starting a small business, you should write a business plan. Writing a business plan is the most important step. This is how people will think about your business. When you are looking for support from a bank, the bank will read your plan seriously before it gives you any help. Even if you're starting the business with your own money, you will still need to have a written plan to help develop your business. The marketing plan is the important part of a business plan. It will help you to sell the products or your services.

Part II Vocabulary and Structure

Section A

16 – 20: CBCAD

21 – 25: DBDAB

Section B

26. cheaper   27. clearly   28. borrowed   29. manager   30. will tell

31. difference   32. be tested   33. meeting   34. personal   35. realized

Part III Reading Comprehension

36 – 40: CAABB

41 – 45: BCCBA

46. bank account   47. cheaper   48. cash machines   49. UK   50. pay

51. I, P   52. K, A   53. G, O   54. M, F   55. H, B

56. 10 years   57. Production Engineers   58. Assistant Works Manager

59. responsible   60. strongly recommend

Part IV Translation

61 – 64: CDCB

65. 感谢你昨天参加在我们办公室里举行的求职面试。我们将在两周内通知你我们对你的申请做出的决定。我们想让你知道，我们将认真考虑你的申请。如果因为某些原因，我们这一次无法为你提供一个职位，那么我们会把你的申请记录在案。一旦有了空缺岗位，我们将会立即通知你。

Part V Writing

66. (1) December 13

(2) 10:30 a.m.

(3) Mr. Peter Margin in APP Company

(4) Manager John Brown

(5) Mr. Peter Margin will go to New York next Monday, so he has no time to meet you next week. Instead, he hopes to see you at 9:30 a.m. this Friday, and at that time talk with you about the details of the cooperation between our two parties. Do you have time at that time? Please call Mr. Peter Margin as soon as possible after reading the message.

(6) Linda Wang

Unit 7

Part I   Listening Comprehension

Directions: *This part is to test your listening ability. It consists of 3 sections.*

Section A

Directions: *This section is to test your ability to understand short dialogues. There are 5 recorded dialogues in it. After each dialogue, there is a recorded question. Both the dialogues and questions will be spoken only once. When you hear a question, you should decide on the correct answer from the 4 choices marked A, B, C and D given in your test paper. Then you should mark the corresponding letter on the Answer Sheet with a single line through the center.*

1. A. Yes, I'd love to.   B. Yes, I think so.
   C. That's all right.   D. It was my pleasure.
2. A. I hate it.   B. Fine.   C. I like it.   D. That's OK.
3. A. It's sunny.   B. You look nice.   C. Nice to see you.   D. I'm 24.
4. A. Too old.   B. Twice a week.   C. 20 kilometers.   D. Two weeks.
5. A. Very nice.   B. I'm hungry.   C. I am full.   D. I think you are right.

Section B

Directions: *This section is to test your ability to understand short conversations. There are 5 recorded conversations in it. After each conversation, there is a recorded question. Both the conversations and questions will be spoken two times. When you hear a question, you should decide on the correct answer from the 4 choices marked A, B, C and D given in your test paper. Then you should mark the corresponding letter on the Answer Sheet with a single line through the center.*

6. A. Doctor and patient.   B. Passenger and ticket collector.
   C. Shop assistant and customer.   D. Boss and clerk.
7. A. It's not important how he dances.   B. It's too crowded to dance away.
   C. If he's careful, no one will notice.   D. No one knows the steps of dancing.

8. A. 400 Yuan.   B. 700 Yuan.
    C. 200 Yuan.   D. 900 Yuan.
9. A. It was too dark.   B. His eyesight is not so good.
    C. The man doesn't want to.   D. He can't find the switch.
10. A. At the railway station.   B. At the airport.
     C. At the police station.   D. At the bank.

Section C

Directions: *In this section you will hear a recorded short passage. The passage is printed on the test paper, but with some words or phrases missing. The passage will be read three times. During the second reading, you are required to put the missing words or phrases on the Answer Sheet in order of the numbered blanks according to what you hear. The third reading is for you to check your writing. Now the passage will begin.*

    Many people have discovered that hobbies can be __11__ as well as fun. Some people have fine __12__ of bottles, flags, stamps or even match boxes.

    Painting, writing and taking photographs are examples of hobbies that may become __13__. Every writer, artist and photographer probably started as a hobbyist before becoming a __14__. Many doctors believe that hobbies help to make our lives more enjoyable. They believe that people who raise fish or collect records are too busy to spend their time worrying. Doctors also think that an active person, such as a football player, should have a __15__ hobby such as reading, while a person who sits at a desk all day should have a lively hobby such as tennis, golf or swimming. Most people in the United States agree with the doctors. It is difficult to find an American who does not have a favorite hobby.

Part II Vocabulary and Structure

Directions: *This part is to test your ability to construct grammatically correct sentences. It consists of 2 sections.*

Section A

Directions: *In this section, there are 10 incomplete sentences. You are required to complete each one by deciding on the most appropriate word or words from the 4 choices marked A, B, C and D. Then you should mark the corresponding letter on the Answer Sheet with a single line through the center.*

16. The train ____ into the station at nine.
     A. pulled   B. dragged   C. hauled   D. pushed
17. All the leaders should attach much importance to their public ____.

A. shape   B. image   C. status   D. figure
18. Our _____ from London to Paris is by way of Dover and Calais.
    A. route   B. way   C. road   D. routine
19. In ____ to the Party's call, a great number of doctors and nurses went to the front line of fighting the flood.
    A. return   B. admission   C. response   D. order
20. They expressed their ____ at being looked down upon by demonstration.
    A. optimism   B. enthusiasm   C. pessimism   D. indignation
21. In interpersonal relations, people should be ____ with each other.
    A. shameful   B. frank   C. reserved   D. indifferent
22. Mary has a bad cold and a ____ throat.
    A. sore   B. painful   C. tender   D. sour
23. His film was a complete failure, which did his reputation a lot of ____.
    A. damage   B. harm   C. injury   D. ruin
24. Every time when I go back to my hometown, I usually spend two days _____ of my relatives.
    A. going the rounds   B. rounding up
    C. making the rounds   D. rounding on
25. Happiness doesn't necessarily ____ money.
    A. go for   B. go through   C. go back   D. go with

Section B

Directions: *There are 10 incomplete statements here. You should fill in each blank with the proper form of the word given in brackets. Write the word or words in the corresponding space on the Answer Sheet.*

26. Give up smoking. Your (healthy) _____ will improve soon.
27. Nothing can (do) _____ unless we are given more information about the situation.
28. (judge) _____ from his cheerful look, I am sure that they have won the game.
29. Both of the twin brothers are capable of doing (technique) _____ work at present.
30. As a public relations officer, he is said (know) _____ some very influential people.
31. The old couple are seen (take) _____ a walk in the park every day after supper.
32. We'd better postpone (discuss) _____ it next week.
33. It is of no much use my (buy) _____ a laptop if you don't like it.
34. I want to rent a more (comfort) _____ room.
35. Not only the students but also their teacher (have) _____ participated in that football game.

Part III Reading Comprehension

Directions: *This part is to test your reading ability. There are 5 tasks for you to fulfill. You should read the reading materials carefully and do the tasks as you are instructed.*

Task 1

Directions: *After reading the following passage, you will find 5 questions or unfinished statements, numbered 36 to 40. For each question or statement there are 4 choices marked A, B, C and D. You should make the correct choice and mark the corresponding letter on the Answer Sheet with a single line through the center.*

When the steam engine was invented in the eighteenth century, it began one of the greatest revolutions that have ever happened in our world. The invention of the petrol engine at the end of the nineteenth century led to another enormous change in our lives. And the computer is almost certainly going to be no less important an invention than these engines were.

Just as there was a Stone Age, an Iron Age and so on, we have been living for centuries in a Paper Age, during which almost all information was kept and sent on paper; and so much of it is wasted after it has been used once that enormous numbers of trees have to be cut down every year to provide us with this paper. But now, with the computer, enormous amounts of information can be stored and sent without any paper at all, using small discs or the Internet.

Computers have made it possible to do very difficult calculations very much faster than any earlier machine could. Computers also allow one to send information to others anywhere in the world, via the telephone line, and to receive information from them. One can send a very long message more quickly from England to Australia, for example, than from one's house to someone in the garden. Computers are not only used for writing; they can produce diagrams and pictures, and they can be used for playing games. One now sees them at airports and railway stations, in hotels and restaurants; in fact, almost everywhere people gather.

36. The author seems to say that the invention of the computer is _____ that of the steam and petrol engines.

    A. less important than   B. far more important than
    C. at least as important as   D. not so important as

37. According to the author, the disadvantage of using paper to keep and send information is that _____.

    A. too many trees are cut down   B. too much paper is needed
    C. it wastes our time   D. it is hard to get enough paper

38. We may infer that the fastest way to send messages is by using _____.

    A. computer   B. air mail   C. discs   D. paper

39. Which of the following functions of the computer is NOT mentioned in the passage?

   A. Offering entertainment.　　　　B. Making phone calls.

   C. Doing office and business work.　　D. Sending information.

40. The title that best expresses the main idea of the passage is _____.

   A. Computer and Our Life　　　　B. Computer and Our Future

   C. Paper Age and Computer Age　　D. Computer Age

Task 2

Directions: *This task is the same as Task 1. The 5 questions or unfinished statements are numbered 41 to 45.*

　　Well, sir, opening a bank account is not very difficult. The trouble is finding the cash to put in it. We at Barclays know there's a student problem—shortage of cash. The monthly cheque from home never seems big enough. We can't make it any bigger but we can make it go a little further. Any student who opens a cheque account with Barclays gets our most important services free. We don't charge you for running your account provided you keep out of the red（有盈余）. You'll find you'll be able to budget（预算） far better when you have a current account. And you'll be able to make payments by cheque or standing order. For example you can ask us to pay your rent directly to your landlady. All you need to do is to make out a standing order, and that means we make sure your rent is paid on time and you don't have to worry about it. You'll receive regular statements to let you know just how you stand. If you have any money problems such as having money sent to you from home, our manager will be pleased to help in any way he can. His experience in money matters is sure to be of value to you.

　　I suggest you open your account today. Don't wait until the term starts — you'll have more than enough to think about then, settling in and starting your studies. You'll be busy arranging your timetable and generally getting used to your new life and new surroundings.

41. A standing order is _____.

   A. a way of notifying a customer how he stands

   B. an instruction to the bank to make regular payments to someone

   C. a way of receiving money regularly

   D. the same as a cheque

42. The student problem the bank knows about is _____.

   A. a student has a lot to do

   B. a student's income is not high enough

   C. the need for advice on money matters

   D. the need for a regular statement

43. It costs a student nothing to run an account provided that _____.

A. he makes his money go further

B. he opens the account before term starts

C. he sees the bank manager about money matters

D. he does not pay out more than he has in the bank

44. The writer of this passage is _____.

   A. a banker
   B. a parent whose son has just gone to college
   C. the president of a university
   D. the chairman of the students' union

45. What is actually offered to the students?

   A. Cash for those who live on their own.
   B. Rent-free housing.
   C. Some free financial services.
   D. A prize for those who study best.

Task 3

Directions: *After reading the following passage, you will find 5 questions or unfinished statements, numbered 46 to 50. For each question or statement there are 4 choices marked A, B, C and D. You should make the correct choice and mark the corresponding letter on the Answer Sheet with a single line through the center.*

Chess must be one of the oldest games in the world. An Arab traveler in India in the year 900 wrote that it was played "long, long ago." Chess was probably invented in India, and it has been played everywhere from Japan to Europe since 1400. The name "chess" is interesting. When one player is attacking the other's king, he says, in English, "check." When the king has been caught and cannot move anywhere, he says "check mate." These words come from Persian. "Shah mat" means "the king is dead." That is when the game is over, and one player has won.

Such an old game changes very slowly. The rules have not always been the same as they are now. For example, at one time the queen could only move one square at a time. Now she is the strongest piece on the board. It would be interesting to know why this has happened! Chess takes time and thought, but it is a game for all kinds of people. You don't have to be a champion in order to enjoy it. It is not always played by two people sitting at the same table. The first time the Americans beat the Russians was in a match played by radio. Some of the chess masters are able to play many people at the same time. The record was when one man played 400 games! It is said that some people play chess by post. This must make chess the slowest game in the world.

46. Which of the following is known to be true?

   A. Chess is an old Indian traveling game.

   B. Chess is the oldest game in the world.

   C. Chess was played in Japan and Europe before 1400.

   D. Chess was played in India long before 900.

47. One player has won the game when _____.

A. he attacks the other's king

B. he says some Persian words

C. the other player's king cannot move anywhere

D. he says "check" to the other player

48. Which of the following will you hear when one player has won the game?
    A. "Shah mat." B. "Check."
    C. "The king is dead." D. "Check mate."

49. Which of the following is NOT correct?

    A. All kinds of people can play chess.

    B. Only two people can play chess sitting at the same table.

    C. Some people write to each other while playing chess.

    D. The Russians lost the game played by radio.

50. According to the old rules of the game _____.

    A. the queen was the strongest piece on the board

    B. the king had to be attacked all the time

    C. the queen could move no more than one square at a time

    D. the king could not move anywhere

Task 4

Directions: *The following is a list of terms related to school education. After reading it, you are required to find the items equivalent to（与……等同）those given in Chinese in the table below. Then you should put the corresponding letters in brackets on the Answer Sheet, numbered 51 through 55.*

A—president B—dean of studies

C—professor D—lecturer

E—Alma Mater F—alumnus

G—student union H—sophomore

I—boarder J—postgraduate

K—compulsory course L—extracurricular activities

M—semester N—credit

O—academic record P—school report

Q—dissertation R—diploma

S—scholarship T—tuition

Examples：（A）校长 （N）学分

51. （ ）校友 （ ）学期

52. （ ）必修课 （ ）成绩单

53. （ ）奖学金 （ ）学生会

54. (   ) 毕业证书   (   ) 课外活动
55. (   ) 教授   (   ) 学费

Task 5

Directions: *The following is a letter. After reading it, you are required to complete the statements that follow the questions (No. 56 to No. 60). You should write your answers in no more than 3 words on the corresponding Answer Sheet.*

April 20th, 1995

Re: Hotel Arrangements for Starways Ltd.

Dear Mr. Hinson,

　　I would like to confirm in writing the arrangements that we agreed last week for the 199 – program.

1. Schedule

A. From 13th May to 16th July, 33 bed nights every Friday and Saturday. Guests will arrive at 18:00 on Friday and depart at 10:00 on Sunday.

B. From 22nd July to 30th August, 66 bed nights every Friday and Saturday, and every Monday and Tuesday.

2. Accommodation

　　For Period A above, we will require 12 standard rooms with shower, and 9 single rooms with shower. For Period B above, we will require 24 standard rooms with shower, and 18 single rooms with shower. The groups will require full American Plan with an additional packed lunch on the day of departure.

　　I hope this represents the discussion we had. I would be grateful if you would let me know if you have any further comments. Meanwhile, I will have a contract drawn up.

　　　　Yours sincerely,

　　　　William Clark

　　　　General Manager

　　　　Parkview Hotel

56. What is this letter about?

　　This letter is about _____ for Starways Ltd.

57. Why did Mr. Clark write this letter?

　　He wrote to _____ that he agreed with Mr. Hinson.

58. When will guests arrive on Friday from 13th May through 16th July?

　　_____.

59. How many single rooms with shower does Mr. Hinson need for Period B?

　　_____.

60. What do the groups require on the day when they depart?

   An _____.

Part IV   Translation

Directions: *This part, numbered 61 through 65, is to test your ability to translate English into Chinese. After each of the sentences numbered 61 to 64, you will read four choices of suggested translation. You should choose the best translation and mark the corresponding letter on your Answer Sheet. And for the paragraph numbered 65, write your translation in the corresponding space on the Translation/Composition Sheet.*

61. When asked to explain what has happened, John was totally at a loss for words.

    A. 要求约翰对发生过的事情进行解释时，他讲的话让人完全摸不着头脑。

    B. 让约翰解释发生过的事情时，约翰完全不知道说什么好。

    C. 由于约翰完全不知道发生过什么事，所以他就让别人解释给他听。

    D. 约翰自己要求要解释发生过的事情，到头来却又一句话也不肯说。

62. Much thought has been given over the recent years to ways of keeping meetings short.

    A. 近年来人们对于控制会议长度的方法提出了很多想法。

    B. 最近几年来人们对于如何减少会议数量提出了很多意见。

    C. 近年来人们对于控制会议长度的方法考虑了很多。

    D. 如何在最近几年内减少会议数量是很多人都曾考虑过的问题。

63. You are no more capable of speaking Spanish than I am.

    A. 你我都不能和西班牙人交流。

    B. 你我都不会说西班牙语。

    C. 你不会说的西班牙语我会说。

    D. 我们会说的西班牙语一样多。

64. It often takes more time and effort to establish a firm in a foreign market than in the domestic one.

    A. 在国外市场建立一家公司比在国内市场建立一家公司往往要花费更多的时间和努力。

    B. 对于一家公司来说，开发国外市场所花费的时间和努力比开发国内市场要多。

    C. 只要能够多花点时间和努力，就可以像在国内市场建立公司一样在国外市场建立公司。

    D. 在国外市场经营一家公司比在国内市场经营一家公司往往要花费更多的时间和努力。

65. John has excellent interpersonal skills and is sociable, patient and a good listener. As a friend, I particularly appreciate his loyalty and sense of humor. I also admire his calmness when facing difficult situations. Therefore, I have no hesitation in recommending him for the position of Training Manager for your company and wish him every success in his application.

Part V Writing

Directions: *This part is to test your ability to do practical writing. You have read the following magazine advertisement in which an American girl is looking for pen-friends and you want to get in touch with her. Write a letter to her (Andy Lewis), telling her about*:

1) *your family*
2) *your schooling or work*
3) *your hobbies*

- Name: Andy Lewis
- Age: 21
- Interest: collecting coins, stamps and postcards, learning foreign languages.
- All letters will be answered.
- Address: 20 Staten Street, Eylandt, DF8 3LF, USA

Unit 7

Part I Listening Comprehension

Section A

1-5: ABCDA

听力原稿

1. Would you like to go to the cinema with me tonight?

2. How are you doing with your computer program?

3. Hello, Mary, I'd like you to meet Mr. Anderson from ABC company.

4. How long can I keep this book?

5. How do you like Chinese food?

Section B

6-10: DACDB

听力原稿

6. W: You were absent from work yesterday, Brown.

   M: I'm terribly sorry I couldn't come. I had a headache.

   Q: What's the relationship between the two speakers?

7. M: I'd love to dance, but I don't know the steps.

   W: It doesn't matter. No one will be looking at us in this crowd.

   Q: What does the woman mean?

8. M: The typewriter costs 900 Yuan but I have only 700 Yuan.

   W: I have 400 Yuan. I can lend you.

   Q: How much does the man have to borrow?

9. W: I think your eyesight is excellent even in the dark. Why don't you turn on the light?

   M: I don't know where the switch is.

   Q: Why doesn't the man turn on the light?

10. M: May I see your air ticket and passport?

　　W: Yes, here you are.

　　Q: Where does the conversation take place?

Section C

11. profitable　　12. collections　　13. occupations　　14. professional　　15. restful

听力原稿

　　Many people have discovered that hobbies can be profitable as well as fun. Some people have fine collections of bottles, flags, stamps or even match boxes.

　　Painting, writing and taking photographs are examples of hobbies that may become occupations. Every writer, artist and photographer probably started as a hobbyist before becoming a professional. Many doctors believe that hobbies help to make our lives more enjoyable. They believe that people who raise fish or collect records are too busy to spend their time worrying. Doctors also think that an active person, such as a football player, should have a restful hobby such as reading, while a person who sits at a desk all day should have a lively hobby such as tennis, golf or swimming. Most people in the United States agree with the doctors. It is difficult to find an American who does not have a favorite hobby.

Part II　Vocabulary and Structure

Section A

16 – 20　ADACD

21 – 25　BABCD

Section B

26. health　　27. be done　　28. Judging　　29. technical　　30. to know

31. to take　　32. discussing　　33. buying　　34. comfortable　　35. has

Part III　Reading Comprehension

36 – 40: CAABD

41 – 45: BBDAC

46 – 50: DCDBC

51. F, M　　52. K, P　　53. S, G　　54. R, L　　55. C, T

56. hotel arrangements　　57. confirm the arrangements　　58. At 18:00　　59. 18

60. additional packed lunch

Part Ⅳ　Translation

61–64：BCBA

65. 约翰有良好的人际沟通能力，喜欢交际，富有耐心，善于倾听。作为他的朋友，我尤其欣赏他的忠实和幽默感。另外，我还很钦佩他面临困境时的镇定。因此，我毫不犹豫地推荐他担任贵公司培训经理一职。祝愿他求职成功。

Part Ⅴ　Writing

Dear Andy,

　　I have read the advertisement and I am very glad to become your pen-friend.

　　I am a girl of 25 years old. I live with my parents in Beijing. I have a brother working in a computer company. I'm a history teacher in a junior middle school. I share the same hobbies with you, and I also like traveling and hiking very much. I usually go camping with my friends on weekends.

　　I like to make friends, not only friends in Beijing, but also friends in other countries. It's a great pleasure to know you. And I am looking forward to hearing from you.

Yours sincerely,
Li Ping

Unit 8

Part I　Listening Comprehension

Directions: *This part is to test your listening ability. It consists of 3 sections.*

Section A

Directions: *This section is to test your ability to give proper responses. There are 5 recorded questions in it. After each question, there is a pause. The questions will be spoken two times. When you hear a question, you should decide on the correct answer from the 4 choices marked A, B, C and D given in your test paper. Then you should mark the corresponding letter on the Answer Sheet with a single line through the center.*

1. A. Thank you.　　　　B. With pleasure.　　　C. Oh, yes.　　　　D. Here you are.
2. A. From 9 a.m. to 6 p.m.　　　　　　　　　B. Far from here.
　　C. Five people.　　　　　　　　　　　　　D. One hundred dollars.
3. A. Please sit down.　B. Take it easy.　　　　C. I'm OK.　　　　D. Yes, of course.
4. A. He's a nice person. B. I work very hard.　 C. You're welcome.　D. Certainly not.
5. A. It's far away.　　 B. It's rather warm.　　C. I hope so.　　　D. I'm afraid I can't.

Section B

Directions: *This section is to test your ability to understand short dialogues. There are 5 recorded dialogues in it. After each dialogue, there is a recorded question. The dialogues and questions will be spoken two times. When you hear a question, you should decide on the correct answer from the 4 choices marked A, B, C and D given in your test paper. Then you should mark the corresponding letter on the Answer Sheet with a single line through the centre.*

6. A. From his friend.　　B. From his teacher.　　C. From his boss.　　D. From his brother.
7. A. Attend a meeting.　B. Hold a party.　　　　C. Take an interview.　D. Meet a friend.
8. A. In the meeting room. B. In her office.　　　C. At home.　　　　D. At the bank.
9. A. It's very boring.　　　　　　　　　　　　 B. That's too busy.

C. She likes it very much.   D. She's going to give it up.
10. A. An engineer.   B. A doctor.   C. A salesman.   D. A secretary.

Section C

Directions: *In this section you will hear a recorded short passage. The passage is printed in the test paper, but with some words or phrases missing. The passage will be read three times. During the second reading, you are required to put the missing words or phrases that you hear on the Answer Sheet in order of the numbered blanks. The third reading is for you to check your writing. Now the passage will begin.*

People visit other countries for many reasons. Some travel ___(11)___ ; others travel to visit interesting places. Whenever you go, for whatever reason, it is important to be ___(12)___. A tourist can draw a lot of attention from local people. Although most of the people you meet are friendly and welcoming, sometimes there are dangers. ___(13)___, your money or passport might be stolen. Just as in your home country, do not expect everyone you meet to be friendly and ___(14)___. It is important to prepare your trip in advance, and ___(15)___ be careful while you are traveling.

Part II Vocabulary and Structure

Directions: *This part is to test your ability to use words and phrases to construct meaningful and grammatically correct sentences. It consists of 2 sections.*

Section A

Directions: *There are 10 incomplete statements here. You are required to complete each statement by choosing the appropriate answer from the 4 choices marked A, B, C and D. You should mark the corresponding letter on the Answer Sheet with a single line through the centre.*

16. The newspaper ____ two people were killed in the accident.
    A. says   B. talks   C. calls   D. asks
17. She told us briefly about how they succeeded in ____ the new product.
    A. develop   B. to develop   C. developed   D. developing
18. The big IT company will ____ a new research center in the city.
    A. set up   B. break up   C. get up   D. turn up
19. I ____ at 130 kilometers per hour when the policeman stopped me.
    A. had driven   B. have driven   C. drive   D. was driving
20. Information about the new system is easy to ____ on the Internet.
    A. like   B. go   C. find   D. open

21. I'd like to introduce you ____ James Stewart, the new manager of our department.
    A. with   B. to   C. of   D. on
22. We had a (n) ____ with him about this problem last night.
    A. explanation   B. impression C. exhibition D. discussion
23. We talked for more than three hours without ____ a cup of tea.
    A. to have   B. having   C. have   D. had
24. They had to give up the plan because they had ____ money.
    A. come up to   B. got along with   C. run out of   D. taken charge of
25. ____ she joined the company only a year ago, she's already been promoted twice.
    A. Although   B. Because   C. If   D. When

Section B

Direction: There are also 10 incomplete statements here. You should fill in each blank with the proper form of the word given in the brackets. Write the word or words in the corresponding space on the Answer Sheet.

26. The new (nation) ____ museum will be open to the public next week.
27. This question is (difficult) ____ than the one I have answered.
28. The secretary has been working for the same (manage) ____ for over 5 years.
29. The hotel, (build) ____ 100 years ago, still looks new.
30. We are pleased to learn that that problem (solve) ____ at yesterday's meeting.
31. I want (point out) ____ that a decision about the matter must be made at once.
32. Although she is young for the job, she is very (experience) ____.
33. The new rules for environmental protection have been (wide) ____ accepted by the public.
34. We demand that the tour guide (tell) ____ us immediately about any change in the schedule.
35. Thank you for your letter of November 15, (invite) ____ us to the trade fair on December 10.

Part III Reading Comprehension

Directions: This part is to test your reading ability. There are 5 tasks for you to fulfill. You should read the reading materials carefully and do the tasks as you are instructed.

Task 1

Directions: After reading the following passage, you will find 5 questions or unfinished statements, numbered 36 to 40. For each question or statement there are 4 choices marked A, B, C and D. You should make the correct choice and mark the corresponding letter on the Answer Sheet with a single line through the center.

Each time we produce a new English dictionary, our aim is always the same: what can we do to make the dictionary more helpful for students of English? As a result of our research with students and discussions with teachers, we decided to focus on providing more examples for this English dictionary.

Examples help students to remember the word they have looked up in the dictionary because it is easier both to remember and to understand a word within a context (上下文). The examples also show that words are often used in many different contexts. For these reasons, we have included 40 per cent more examples in this new book.

We edit all the examples to remove difficult words and to make sure they are easier to understand.

We very much hope this new book will be of use not only to the students of English but also to the teachers.

36. The aim of the author in producing this new dictionary is to ____.
    A. correct mistakes in the old dictionary   B. make it more helpful for students
    C. increase the number of words   D. add pictures and photos

37. A word is easier to remember and understand if it is ____.
    A. included in a word list   B. pronounced correctly
    C. explained in English   D. used in a context

38. What is special about this new dictionary?
    A. It is small and cheap.   B. It has a larger vocabulary.
    C. It has 40% more examples.   D. It is designed for students and teachers.

39. The purpose of removing difficult words in the examples is to ____.
    A. make them easier to understand   B. provide more useful words
    C. introduce more contexts   D. include more examples

40. The passage is most probably taken from ____.
    A. a letter to the editor   B. a comment on a novel
    C. an introduction to a dictionary   D. a news-report in the newspaper

Task 2

Directions: *This task is the same as Task 1. The 5 questions or unfinished statements are numbered 41 through 45.*

What is the better way of staying away from the cold winter days? Come out to our Hall Markets in the beautiful countryside, full of color, fun, music and delicious food! With over 350 stalls (摊位) selling wonderful home-made and home-grown goods, this will surely be a great day out.

The Hall Markets are held on the first Sunday of each month from 10:00 am to 3:00 pm at Hall Village. They are operated by Hartley Lifecare Co. Ltd. All the income will go to help and support service for people with disabilities (残疾).

Volunteers (志愿者) play an important part in the success and pleasant atmosphere at the Hall Markets. Hartley Lifecare is always grateful to have you serve as volunteers with the Hall Markets.

If you are interested in being one of our volunteers and spending a few hours with us each month, please contact us during business hours on 6260 5555.

41. According to the passage, the Hall Markets are held ____.
    A. in the countryside   B. to attract volunteers
    C. to promote winter sales   D. by people with disabilities
42. There are over 350 stalls in the Hall Markets that ____.
    A. are operated by the disabled B. offer free food to volunteers
    C. sell home-made goods   D. are open day and night
43. The income made by the Hall Markets goes to ____.
    A. expand Hartley Lifecare Co. Ltd.   B. support service for the disabled
    C. create more fun for customers   D. develop local economy
44. When are the Hall Markets open?
    A. The first Sunday of each month.   B. Every day from 10 am to 3 pm.
    C. The first day of each month.   D. Every weekend in winter.
45. This passage is written for the purpose of inviting ____.
    A. tourists   B. villagers   C. businessmen   D. volunteers

Task 3

Directions: *The following is a letter. After reading it, you should complete the information by filling in the blanks marked 46 through 50 in no more than 3 words in the table below.*

2 November 2008

Dear Dr. Yamata,

The Association of Asian Economic Studies is pleased to invite you to be this year's guest speaker at its annual international symposium (研讨会). The symposium will be held for 3 days from December 22nd to 24th, 2008. This year's topic will be Economic Development in Asia. About 100 people from various countries will be attending the symposium. They would be pleased to meet you and share their views with you.

The Association will cover all the expenses of your trip to this symposium.

As the program is to be announced on December 1st, 2008, will you kindly let us know before that time whether your busy schedule will allow you to attend our symposium? We are looking forward to your favorable reply.

Yours sincerely,
John Smith
Secretary of Association of Asian Economic Studies

Letter of Invitation

Writer of the letter: _____(46)_____

Organizer of the Symposium: Association of _____(47)_____

Guest speaker to be invited: Dr. Yamata

Starting date of the symposium: _____(48)_____

Number of guests invited: about _____(49)_____

Topic of the symposium: _____(50)_____ in Asia

Task 4

Directions: *The following is a list of terms. After reading it, you are required to find the items equivalent to（与……等同）those given in Chinese in the table below. Then you should put the corresponding letters in the brackets on the Answer Sheet, numbered 51 through 55.*

A—after-sales service   B—business license
C—business risk   D—dead stock
E—department store   F—import license
G—limited company   H—net weight
I—packing charge   J—price tag
K—purchasing power   L—seller's market
M—shipping date   N—shopping rush
O—show window   P—supermarket
Q—trade agreement

Examples: （D）滞销品   （I）包装费
  51. （   ）净重   （   ）百货商店
  52. （   ）购买力   （   ）商业风险
  53. （   ）超级市场   （   ）卖方市场
  54. （   ）有限公司   （   ）售后服务
  55. （   ）装船日期   （   ）进口许可证

Task 5

Directions: *The following is an advertisement. After reading it, you are required to complete the statements that follow the questions (No. 56 to No. 60). You should write your answers in no more than 3 words on the corresponding Answer Sheet.*

Grounds-person（场地管理员）Wanted

The Yanton Playingfield Committee has for many years been fortunate to have Eddie Christiansen as grounds-person at its sports ground in Littlemarsh. However, after 10 years of service, Eddie has decided it's time to retire in July. The committee wishes him the best for his retired life.

However, this leaves us needing a new grounds-person. This role is part-time, averaging around 5 hours per week. The duties involve the mowing（除草）, rolling, and trimming（修剪）of the field edges. Applicants（求职人）need to be able to drive and use the equipment needed for the above-mentioned duties.

Applicants can either contact Hugh Morris, 42 Spencer Avenue, tel. 765 – 4943780, to discuss or register an interest in the position, or any member of the Playingfield Committee.

56. Which organization is in need of a grounds-person?

    The _____.

57. Why is a new grounds-person needed?

    Because the former grounds-person, Eddie Christiansen, has decided it's time to _____.

58. What are the duties of a grounds-person?

    His duties involve the mowing, _____ of the field edges.

59. What should applicants be able to do?

    They should be able to _____ the equipment needed for the duties.

60. Who is the contact person?

    _____ or any committee member.

Part IV Translation

Directions: This part, numbered 61 to 65, is to test your ability to translate English into Chinese. Each of the four sentences (NO. 61 to No. 64) is followed by four choices of suggested translation marked A, B, C and D. Make the best choice and write the corresponding letter on the Answer Sheet. Write your translation of the paragraph (No. 65) in the corresponding space on the Translation/ Composition Sheet.

61. Seldom can people find international news on the front page of this popular local newspaper.

    A. 人们不会在这份地方报纸前几页上寻找重要的国际新闻。

    B. 人们很难在当地这份深受欢迎的报纸头版看到国际新闻。

    C. 人们从这份当地发行的报纸第一页上几乎找不到国际新闻。

    D. 人们阅读当地放心的报刊时从不查看头版刊登的国际新闻。

62. The function of e-commerce is more than just buying and selling goods and services on the Internet.

A. 电子商务的功能很多，如提供网上货物交易的服务。

B. 电子商务更多的功能在于做买卖并提供网络服务。

C. 电子商务的功能不只是在互联网上买卖货物和服务。

D. 电子商务的功能更多的是从互联网上买卖货物和服务。

63. All flights have been cancelled because of the snowstorm, so many passengers could do nothing except take the train.

A. 暴风雪使所有航班被取消，许多乘客只能改乘火车。

B. 所有的航班因暴风雪而取消，许多乘客也无法改乘火车。

C. 受暴风雪影响，许多乘客坚持改乘火车，因此所有航班被迫取消。

D. 由于暴风雪的影响，许多乘客不得不放弃乘坐飞机，而改乘火车。

64. This new type of air-conditioner is so energy-efficient that it can save the company forty thousand dollars a year.

A. 这种新型空调功率很高，公司电费一年高达四万美元。

B. 这种新型空调高效节能，一年能为公司节省四万美元。

C. 这种新型空调效率很高，公司一年节省了电费四万美元。

D. 这种新型空调效率很高，公司一年仅需支付电费四万美元。

65. The ABC Railway Company has greatly improved its public hotline service. Simply dial 3929 – 3499 to get information about all the services of the company. The telephone information system is working to serve you 24 hours all year round. The customer service staff （员工） are also ready to provide you with the information you need. Their service hours are from Monday to Sunday, 7：00 am to 9：00 pm.

Part V   Writing

Directions：*This part is to test your ability to do practical writing. You are required to write a letter of thanks based on the following information given in Chinese. Remember to do your writing on the Composition/Translation Sheet.*

说明：假定你是 JKM 公司的 Thomas Black，刚从巴黎（Paris）出差回来，请给在巴黎的 Jane Costa 小姐写一封感谢信。

写信日期：2008 年 12 月 21 日

内容：

1. 感谢她在巴黎期间的热情接待；

2. 告诉她巴黎给你留下了美好的印象，你非常喜欢法国的……，参观工厂和学校后学到了很多……；

3. 期待再次与她见面。

注意：必须包括对收信人的称谓、写信日期、发信人的签名等基本格式。

Unit 8

Part I Listening Comprehension

Section A

1-5：CADAB

听力原稿

1. Excuse me, are you Mr. Smith from America?

2. Mr. Johnson, when is the library open?

3. It's rather hot today, would you please open the window?

4. What do you think of your boss?

5. What's the weather like in your city?

Section B

6-10：DDBCA

听力原稿

6. W: Are you coming for the basketball game?

   M: Yes, I've got a ticket from my brother.

   Q: Where did the man get the ticket?

7. M: Can you stay for dinner?

   W: I'd love to, but I have to go to meet a friend at the airport.

   Q: What's the woman going to do?

8. W: I'm here to see Miss Brown.

   M: Miss Brown? Oh, she is in her office.

   Q: Where is Miss Brown?

9. M: Do you like your new job?

   W: Yes, I like it very much.

   Q: How does the woman feel about her new job?

10. W: Did you work as a salesman in that company?

M: No, I was an engineer.

Q: What did the man do in that company?

Section C

11. on business   12. safe   13. For example   14. helpful   15. always

People visit other countries for many reasons. Some travel on business; others travel to visit interesting places. Whenever you go, for whatever reason, it is important to be safe. A tourist can draw a lot of attention from local people. Although most of the people you meet are friendly and welcoming, some times there are dangers. For example, your money or passport might be stolen. Just as in your home country, do not expect everyone you meet to be friendly and helpful. It is important to prepare your trip in advance, and always be careful while you are traveling.

Part II Vocabulary and Structure

Section A

16-20: ADADC

21-25: BDBCA

Section B

26. national   27. more difficult   28. manager   29. built   30. was solved

31. to point out   32. experienced   33. widely   34. (should) tell   35. inviting

Part III Reading Comprehension

36-40: BDCAC

41-45: ACBAD

46. John Smith   47. Asian Economic Studies   48. December 22nd   49. 100

50. Economic Development

51. H, E   52. K, C   53. P, L   54. G, A   55. M, F

56. Yanton Playingfield Committee

57. retire

58. rolling and trimming

59. drive and use

60. Hugh Morris

Part Ⅳ Translation-English into Chinese

61 – 64：BCAB

65. ［译文］ABC 铁路公司极大地改善了公司的公众热线服务。您只需简单拨打 3929 – 3499 就可以获得公司所有的服务信息。电话信息系统常年 24 小时为您服务。客户人工服务也将随时为您提供您需要的信息，人工服务的时间是周一到周日早上七点到晚上九点。

［解析］该段文字是对于某公司电话服务系统的介绍，由五个句子组成。在翻译此题过程中应注意以下几点：其中第一个句子的 public hotline service 意为"公众热线服务"，不要译为"公共热线服务"。第二个句子是祈使句，要注意翻译句子时的语气。第三个句子要注意词组 all year around 的翻译。第四个句子中含有一个定语从句 information you need 意为"您需要的信息"。最后一个句子注意时间的表达方法。

Part Ⅴ Writing

参考范文

December 21st, 2008

Dear Miss Jane Costa,

I'm writing to thank you for your warm hospitality while I was on business in Paris. （感谢的原因）If it had not been for your assistance I would not have a very enjoyable time there. （对方给你的具体帮助以及没有对方帮助时的后果）

Paris has given me a very pleasant impression. It's unforgettable. And I also like the people and food there. At the same time I learned a great deal after visiting factories and schools. （给出细节）Again, I'd like to express my warm （thanks）gratitude to you and look forward to seeing you soon.

Yours sincerely
Thomas Black
JKM Company